ALAN BUTLER has written everything from comedy plays for the BBC to an Elizabethan novel, but his greatest love is history. Some years ago, on holiday in Crete, he came across the archaeological artefact known as the Phaistos Disc and recognized it immediately as some sort of astronomical or astrological calendar. His increasing obsession with the disc culminated in his writing *The Bronze Age Computer Disc*. His most recent book, *Civilization One: The World Is Not as You Thought It Was*, was co-written with Christopher Knight, co-author of *The Hiram Key*.

STEPHEN DAFOE is a freelance writer, author and publisher who lives in Hinton, Alberta, near Canada's Jasper National Park. He entered the Masonic fraternity in 1992 and is the author of a number of books including *Unholy Worship*, which examines the history of the Knights Templar. He appears frequently in television documentaries, has created numerous websites, and is often called on to address Masonic lodges.

The Knights Templar Revealed

Alan Butler and Stephen Dafoe

HODDER

HODDER AUSTRALIA

Published in Australia and New Zealand in 2006
by Hodder Australia
(An imprint of Hachette Livre Australia Pty Limited)
Level 17, 207 Kent Street, Sydney NSW 2000
Website: www.hachette.com.au

First published in the UK by Constable & Robinson Ltd 2006

ISBN 0 7336 2121 X

Cover photography courtesy of Getty and Corbis
Cover design by Nick Castle
Text design by George Palmer
Printed in the European Union

Contents

Chapter 1

Orthodox and Unorthodox Traditions

As the autumn sun painted the eastern horizon at dawn all across France on Friday, 13 October 1307, there came a loud knocking on the stout oak doors of numerous Knights Templar presbyteries. The forces of Philip IV, King of France, had been mobilized to undertake a dawn raid on the various establishments administered by the White Knights throughout the entire kingdom. With ruthless efficiency, the seneschal of the king arrested any knight, sergeant or servant found on Templar property, and an extensive search was mounted for any Templar personnel who might have managed to slip away in the ensuing confusion.

This ended, history relates, one of the most successful military, commercial and fiscal organizations the medieval world ever knew. Within hours, the inquisitors were extracting almost unbelievable admissions of every imaginable sort of heinous crime and religious heresy from the unfortunate men who had fallen to their state-sanctioned barbarism. Very soon, Templar brothers were facing executioners in many parts of the kingdom whilst others were thrown into dark dungeons, never to see the light of day again. A tame pope, tied inextricably to the apron strings of an avaricious French king, was soon forced to issue an edict that would abolish the Order of the Templar Knights across the whole of Europe and beyond. Assets were seized, more brothers were arrested and an attempt was made to eradicate the memory of the Templar Knights from history.

Eventually, Jacques de Molay, the grand master of the "Poor Knights of Christ and the Temple of Solomon", was roasted slowly over a spit on a small island outside the city of Paris and the fabulous Knights Templar had gone forever.

As the acrid smoke drifted up into the Paris sky, it carried with it the hopes and aspirations of an extraordinary organization that had, in slightly less than two centuries, altered forever the world of which it was part.

The Knights Templar had been formed in the early decades of the twelfth century as a result of a small band of poor and bedraggled knights who had turned up, footsore and weary, at the gate of the palace of Baudoin II, King of Jerusalem. They begged his indulgence and declared that it was their avowed intention to guard the lives and property of Christian pilgrims who, following the success of the First Crusade, were making their way in droves from the coast of Palestine to the holy shrines of Jerusalem.

Baudoin received these selfless soldiers for Christ with open arms. Just over a decade later they returned to their native France where they were converted into an official order by sanction of Pope Honorius II and later were advanced by the Cistercian Pope Innocent II. Adopted by the Cistercians, a brand new offshoot of the Benedictine monastic endeavour, they were given a series of rules to govern their activities, both in the Levant and wherever else they were to be found. They would be the true "soldiers of Christ" and would carry the fame of their courage, fighting acumen and willingness to die for God far across foreign lands.

The idea proved popular. Recruits and offers of money and land came flowing in from far and wide. Soon, numerous presbyteries, castles, farms and churches were built and occupied by the Templar knights and their servants. The

Templars fitted out ships, creating both a merchant and fighting navy. In time they became the most famous warriors, travellers, bankers and financiers of their day.

With the loss of the Holy Land to the Malmukes toward the end of the thirteenth century, the Templars consolidated their holdings in Europe and beyond. They not only continued to grow in size, but also in arrogance and greed. Soon the word "Templar" became synonymous with pride, avarice and cruelty, so that barely an individual who fell within the remit of their numerous activities had a good word to say for them. The phrase "to drink like a Templar" was a common expression among the populace and a fitting example of the disrespect shown towards the order in the latter days.

Eventually, it fell to the lot of King Philip, known in his own lifetime as Philip the Fair, to eradicate this heretical and corrupt cancer from the body of the developing Europe, and this he attempted to do on that fateful day in October 1307. This, then, is the story as we both first learned it from any one of hundreds of orthodox books on the history of the period and, with a few modifications, it is still the tale to which most historians resort. But it surely cannot be the whole truth for within the pages of hundreds of more fanciful excursions into history we discover a completely different sort of Templar knights, whose reputation seems based far more on myth than reality. These peerless white-mantled saviours are the stuff of medieval Arthurian legend, and indeed many have claimed them to be the true source of such tales. As protector of the poor, true champion of God, perhaps even legatee of a secret arcane wisdom, the mythical Templar exemplifies loyalty, humanity, perseverance and genuine humility. Historians deny his existence (and we doubt it). But what we never doubted was that the truth of the Templar story was likely to be infinitely more complicated than either the traditionalists or the esotericists had realized.

Our initial research showed conclusively that the Templars were, of necessity, intricately wound into the web of history of which they were destined to become a part. There was much of the mythological about accounts related to their meteoric rise to stardom in the black sky of medieval Europe, but these could not detract from the genuine and provable accomplishments of the knightly order. They clearly had been the best merchants of their day, and it was obvious that they had "invented" cheque-book banking and that they sowed the seeds of the later capitalism upon which the economy of practically the whole world is presently based.

Each of us had approached the story of the Knights Templar from entirely different standpoints, and so we were quite surprised to discover that even at our first meeting, a little more than a year prior to the writing of these words, we were starting to reach the same sort of conclusions. As a result, our respective research had brought us to a position from which it was possible to make a list of common conclusions, even if at that time we could not prove the many assertions that sprang from them:

1. The established and often accepted story of the sudden and quite "casual" formation of the Knights Templar could not be the truth.
2. The Order of the Poor Knights of Christ and the Temple of Solomon was "blood-tied" to other important and powerful factions working within the Europe of their day.
3. The Knights Templar almost certainly had a motivation and an intention in their existence, the truth of which lay far beyond the estimation of orthodox scholars.
4. Their demise was not as complete as contemporary sources had wished a credulous world to believe.
5. The accusations of heresy levelled at the Templars at the time of the 1307 attacks were not entirely without foundation. In other words, we were both already of the opinion that the Knights Templar were definitely not following the orthodox teachings of the Roman Catholic Church of their day.

Armed with these realizations, and bolstered by a wealth of evidence that we had collected respectively, we set out on a search to discover the truth underpinning this most extraordinary institution. Our first discovery, as we suspected, was that no matter how unlike contemporary organizations throughout Europe the Templars may have been, their story could not be taken in isolation. In other words their existence was funded by the development of medieval Europe and so they had to be an intrinsic part of it. We believed, and still believe, that any attempt to view the Knights Templar in isolation is therefore doomed to inevitable failure. This was especially true in light of co-author Alan Butler's previous research, which he had arrived at after extensive examination of Templar existence and imperatives at the end of a long excursion into much more ancient European history. A brief explanation of Alan's earlier research will be necessary if the reader is to understand the position which the founders of this most extraordinary fraternity occupied within European society at the commencement of the twelfth century.

Alan had been looking at the complex and fascinating world associated with the mathematical, astronomical and geometrical knowledge of Bronze Age Europeans. In his book *The Bronze Age Computer Disc*, Alan had focused his attention on the Phaistos Disc, an artefact discovered in Crete at the beginning of the twentieth century. Discovered in the ruins of the Minoan Palace of Phaistos in southern Crete, this small, baked clay Disc was dated to about 1800 BC (a representation of it can be seen on the cover of the book). The Phaistos Disc resides today in the Heraklion Museum in Crete, where thousands of puzzled museum-goers stare at it every year. The Phaistos Disc is composed on each side of an incised spiral within which lie groups of mysterious pictographs or hieroglyphic inscriptions. These are generally naturalistic in composition and were originally carved onto "dyes" which were then pressed into the wet clay of the Disc.

Nobody has ever been able to satisfactorily ascertain the meaning of the hieroglyphs on the Disc, though many scholars have tried and a few claim to have achieved a degree of success.

The basic problem lies in the fact that there is no comparison between these hieroglyphic characters and any other script in use at the time. This fact, taken together with the realization that the language used by the Minoans on Crete is not known, effectively means that a reliable and universally accepted interpretation of the meaning of the Phaistos Disc, in a linguistic sense, is very unlikely to emerge.

But Alan approached the problem from a different direction. He was looking for the proof of an ancient calendar which logic had already told him must once have existed in prehistoric Europe. This calendar, he suggested, must have been based on a ritual year that was considered to be of 366 days in length, probably reflecting a form of proto geometry which contained circles considered to be comprised of 366 degrees.

The problem with such a calendar (in fact any calendar) was that it would soon run out of sequence with the true Earth year, which is actually around 365.25 days in length. There have been many calendars used by humanity in various cultures and historical periods, but however they work, they must have built into them compensations of one sort or another which will constantly bring them into line with the "actual" time duration of the Earth's passage around the Sun. Calendars are of great use to agriculturists who need to have an understanding, year on year, of the most propitious times to plant crops. If the ritual calendar used by such farmers does not broadly follow the true solar calendar, planting times will begin to "drift" throughout the year with potentially disastrous results. In the case of our own civilization, we have eventually opted for the ritual use of a 365-day year which demands the addition of an extra day every four years (plus certain other more refined compensations) in order to keep it in tune with the real state of the Sun/Earth relationship.

Alan discovered that the mathematical cycles inferred by the "number" of hieroglyphs on each side of the Phaistos Disc suggested a method by which a ritual calendar of 366 days could be reconciled with the true solar year. In this case the procedure would be to follow a second calendar based on cycles of 123 days. After 4 such cycles (492 days), 1 day would be removed from the ritual 366-day calendar. In this way the ritual calendar would remain in tune with the solar year for well in excess of 3,700 years before any other compensation would need to be made. In the end, the Phaistos Disc provided a second calendar that was too precise and indicated a number system far cleverer than would have been required to reconcile ritual and solar years. It became obvious that the compensations indicated by the Phaistos Disc related to a sacred geometry which comprised 366 degrees to the circle, as opposed to our modern one of 360 degrees.

Thus it was that Alan gradually began to rebuild the fascinating geometrical, astronomical and mathematical knowledge of the ancient Minoans. Realizing that they had also clearly been dealing in linear measurement, he cast around for a truly ancient scale of measurement that might fit the system. This he found far from Crete, in the British Isles. The late Professor Alexander Thom, an engineer from Oxford University, worked tirelessly for many decades, carefully surveying and measuring the many megalithic standing stones, stone circles and other alignments left on the landscape of Britain and parts of France since truly ancient times. One important fact emerged as a result of such tireless efforts. Almost every monument, dating from at least 3500 BC until around 1500 BC, had been built using the same basic linear measurement. This, Professor Thom discovered, was on average 82.96656 cm in length and he named it the "megalithic yard".

When applied to the geometry and mathematics that Alan had discovered in Crete, it became obvious that the megalithic yard was part of a mathematical "world view" that had perpetuated across a vast period of time and throughout large areas of Europe. With the aid of the megalithic yard and the geometry of which it was an intrinsic part, the ancient peoples of Britain, and locations much further afield, must have had an astounding knowledge of the true dimensions of the Earth upon which they lived. All these matters are discussed at length in Alan's book *The Bronze Age Computer Disc* and readers wishing a more complete explanation of the entire principle are advised to consult this work.

Soon after finishing *The Bronze Age Computer Disc*, Alan chanced across the little known work of a French researcher who had been active in the early part of the twentieth century. His name was Xavier Guichard and in his book, *Eleusis (Alaises)*, published in the 1930s, he had made some startling claims. Guichard believed that parts of western Europe had once been covered by a series of long straight lines, sometimes running for many kilometres across the landscape. Many of these, he maintained, commenced at central "hubs" and radiated outward, like the spokes of a bicycle wheel. Guichard claimed that the true "run" of the lines could be ascertained because all along the lines were settlements which contained place names of a very specific type. All the place names in question contained an "al" component, for example "Alaise", "Calaise", "Falaise" and the like. The "al" component, Guichard believed, was the remnant of the Greek word "*hal*", which means salt. Guichard thought therefore that these lines across the landscape had been a form of navigation most probably used from the early transportation of salt from one place to another.

In addition to the radiating "bicycle spoke" lines, Guichard also claimed to have found another, completely different, set of lines. These were very much like the modern lines of longitude and latitude to be found on any map. Once again these were liberally sprinkled with the "al" place names, but unlike modern lines of longitude and latitude, they were not exactly 1 modern degree of arc apart. Guichard's lines, particularly the longitudinal ones, were almost exactly 59 modern minutes of arc apart, and he explained this fact by suggesting that the people creating them had not been sufficiently adept in their knowledge of Earth geometry or in their surveying techniques.

To Alan the answer to this anomaly came almost immediately.

If, as he already suspected, our Bronze Age ancestors had considered the Earth to be split into 366 divisions, and not 360, then it stood to reason that longitudinal lines would be very slightly closer together. The expectation was that they would occur at just over 59 modern minutes of arc apart, which was exactly the case with regard to the longitudinal lines discovered by Xavier Guichard. It was also a fact that the period during which Guichard claimed the lines had been laid down was contemporary with the use of the megalithic yard and in the same geographical areas. Guichard claimed that the main longitudinal line in this system had been placed at what today would be considered 6 degrees east of Greenwich.

Working westward from France, Alan plotted Guichard's expectations for the longitudinal lines on Britain, which Guichard himself had never done. There was no doubt that the same system had existed in Britain too because the proliferation of "al" type place names was exactly the same. A further review of the lines also showed that countless burials, standing stones, stone circles and alignments of all imaginable sorts, and from the same historical period, had also been placed on or near to these longitudinal lines on the living landscape. Alan decided to call the lines "Salt Lines" in deference to the lifelong efforts of Xavier Guichard, who had never achieved any scientific credibility for his monumental efforts.

The most surprising aspect to Salt Line research lay in the fact that it soon became obvious that the run of these lines, though actually invisible on the ground, had retained a mystical significance for countless centuries after those creating the lines had ceased to exist. The Celts, probably moving into Britain after about 500 BC, had shown a great reverence for the Salt Lines and had placed many shrines and sacred sites upon them. This had also been true in the case of the Romans and, later, the Anglo-Saxons. For quite some time it seemed as though these successive races may have simply been revering places that were already considered to be sacred at the time of their arrival in Britain. However, it eventually became apparent that each culture had created brand new sites on the run of the Salt Lines in positions where there was absolutely no evidence of an earlier edifice.

Alan deeply suspected that there was no real chance of proving that successive cultures arriving in Britain had actually placed their own burials and religious shrines in locations on Salt Line runs that had not previously been revered. However, a test did show itself as workable with regard to the later Normans, a section of who also appeared to have understood the Salt Line system very well back in their native Normandy.

Alan reasoned that any individual occupying what may have been considered to be a ritually significant Salt Line site in his or her native Normandy would probably strive to do the same when arriving in Britain after the Norman Conquest of 1066, at which time England was effectively taken over by the Normans. A full list of knights fighting alongside William of Normandy in Hastings in 1066 made it possible to ascertain the points of origin of many of William's underlings. A list was made of all of those who had occupied Salt Line holdings in Normandy or France. It remained to discover what proportion of these people also gained Salt Line lands in England. The results were not in doubt and showed that there was an overwhelming likelihood that those lords emanating from Salt Line holdings on the Continent were very much more likely than chance to obtain and settle on Salt Line holdings in England too.

It was whilst studying these very powerful French and Norman baronial families that Alan started to come across the names of individuals who had played an important part in the prosecution of the First Crusade, which captured Jerusalem for Christianity in 1099. These same families, and other Salt Line families who were blood-tied to them, had been instrumental in the formation of the Cistercian monastic order and that of the Knights Templar.

This information offered a different "window" on the probable motives of such family groups and also tied in well with other independent evidence regarding the theme which we shall explore more as our evidence unfolds. All the way through the story of megalithic geometry, astronomy and mathematics, and also related to the laying down of the Salt Lines, a religious imperative was evident. This ultimately applied to the Cistercians and the Knights Templar, and an intriguing series of possibilities began to unfold.

Co-author Stephen Dafoe already had one of the broadest evidence bases available relating to the Knights Templar, and we pooled our resources to verify our premises regarding this surprisingly little understood institution that had previously been missed by researchers who were not party to our own observations and discoveries. The results were immediate and far-reaching. Some of these we itemized in our first book on the theme, *The Warriors and the Bankers*, published by Templar Books in 1998. It is our intention in what follows to amplify on those findings and bring an even greater degree of corroboration to bear on these matters.

Our finding regarding the ultimate, genuine fate of the Knights Templar is becoming widely known since the aim of *The Warriors and the Bankers* was to explore what happened to the Templars after the pivotal year of 1307. However, we soon began to realize that even this knowledge was only a small part of what was really available because we had never addressed the circumstances leading up to the period in which the Templars were actually formed. To do so adequately, we need to travel back in time about 6,000 years to a period when the established hunter-gatherers of western Europe were turning their attention towards the possibility of a more settled existence based upon farming. For it became evident to us, no matter how unlikely the scenario might seem, that the most obvious and common link between the Templars, the Cistercians and the megalithic peoples was a humble and historically understated domestic animal, the sheep.

Chapter 2

A Garden of Eden

Unlike other wild animals that would come to be domesticated by our most ancient forebears, the sheep's ancestors were not present in Britain or France for a protracted period prior to the rise of the megalithic cultures of the late Stone Age and Bronze Age. The wild sheep was a creature whose home ranges had encompassed parts of the Middle East, a section of North Africa, the Balkans and some of the islands of the eastern Mediterranean. Its earliest domestication was probably in what is today known as Turkey, though there can be no certainty about this fact. What is likely is that the sheep was already herded and bred by farmers as long ago as 8000 BC, a product of peoples who also experimented with cereal crops and other domesticated wild plants. In addition to the sheep, wild cattle and pigs were being tamed and reared.

It was much later that such practices became widespread further west. For some time after the retreat of the glaciers and the end of the last Ice Age, the peoples of France and Britain retained an essentially "hunter-gatherer" culture, and this way of life is unlikely to have given rise to any widespread dependence on farming until around 4000 BC. We know little of these people or their racial origins, but Alan's research into the

Phaistos Disc, and subsequently the use of the megalithic astronomical, geometrical and mathematical systems, shows that they must have been in contact, at some time, with contemporary peoples living much further to the east in Crete. Alan was able to show that there was an affinity of knowledge between the peoples of what are now Britain and France and the culture on Crete that has become known to us as that of the Minoans.

Although using a slightly different system of linear measurements, which are based on the "Minoan foot" which is 30.36 cm in length, the whole Minoan mathematical worldview is essentially megalithic in origin. The Minoan foot represents the base of a measuring system that must originally have been rooted in the same one that spawned the megalithic yard. The reasoning behind this assertion is explained in detail in *The Bronze Age Computer Disc* but essentially responds to the fact that 1,000 Minoan feet are exactly the same linear distance as 366 megalithic yards. The megalithic yard is much older however and was certainly in use in Britain as early as 3500 BC, at which time the Minoan civilization was still a full thousand years short of its ultimate emergence. Since there is little or no evidence of the existence of the megalithic system within central or southern Europe, the inference must surely be that the Minoan civilization ultimately responded to ideas that had originally emerged much further west.

The principles of megalithic geometry and mathematics underpinned a rich religious tradition and this was certainly the case in Minoan Crete. Evidence to bolster this assertion in the case of such an early stage in the history of Britain and France is scant. However, it may be reasonably safe to assume that such similar mathematical and astronomical practices shared by two such early cultures probably indicate a broad similarity of underlying belief. Minoan Crete became Europe's first super-civilization and the rich vein of archaeology left behind by these most fascinating people has left us with a generally good understanding of the beliefs and practices of the people concerned.

This aspect of our research we will return to in the fullness of time.

What concerns us initially is the underlying fabric of Minoan life which was based on extremely sophisticated farming techniques considering the early period in question. As early as 2000 BC a fairly complex culture had begun to develop on the island, probably for a number of different reasons.

1. Crete is a fairly remote island and once its people reached a reasonably high degree of sophistication, it is doubtful that incursions of foreign adversaries would have proved to be successful against an entrenched, cohesive and determined populace. In any case no such early culture had sufficient maritime acumen to launch a potentially successful invasion.
2. Crete is a virtual Garden of Eden, with a wealth of different wild crops that were ripe for domestication. At the time humans first arrived, it contained a wealth of animal species such as ferocious wild cattle, goats, sheep and possibly wild pigs. Probably no area of Europe provided a better potential base for the emergence of an early civilization than the verdant island of Crete.
3. The embryonic population of the island comprised the less warlike Europeans of the neolithic period, races that are not earmarked by experts as having been overtly violent or "martial" in their general way of life. This fact probably fostered a better early co-operation, which eventually gave way to the founding of a cohesive and successful economy.

The form of culture that developed on Crete is virtually without parallel in the ancient world, though its actual composition is still not totally understood. What we do know is that Minoan life centred on any one of several different palace complexes. The largest of these was situated at Knossos, which is to the north of Crete, centrally placed and not far from the ocean. Here a whole succession of palaces was built, each one larger and more splendid than its predecessor. Whether Knossos represented the throne of a monarch we cannot be certain for the Minoans, unlike their contemporaries the Egyptians, have left no massive statuary, friezes or steles to eulogize a god-like monarchy. In terms of pictographic art the Minoans created fabulous wall frescos and a good deal of attractive and vibrant pottery. In each case we may get glimpses of a courtly elite (obviously comprising people of refinement and sensitivity), together with an obvious passion for nature in all its forms.

In terms of naturalistic designs the Minoans were fond of all types of flowers and a range of animal themes. They often depicted marine life, such as dolphins, octopus and fish, and seem to have been always ready to drink in, and then portray with artistic abandon, the natural world of which they were a part.

For a people with such fineness of touch, the Minoans proved to be wonderfully adept at monumental building projects. The surviving ruins of the palace of Knossos, and indeed those of Phaistos, Malia and Zakro, show the Minoans to have been excellent builders whose exploits in balanced columns, the use of light-wells, dividable rooms and multistorey techniques would not see the light of day again for many centuries. In the case of the very extensive palace of Knossos, it is clear that the whole complex was built after first answering the inevitable questions regarding drainage and sewage disposal (not generally considered to be of paramount importance to many early civilizations). Indeed one of the inner rooms of the palace of Knossos contains what may be the world's first flushing toilet, which must have looked very much like a thoroughly modern example.

The palace was serviced by a number of freshwater springs. It was a light and airy place to live and probably surrounded, in its heyday, by ornamental gardens. The achievements of Minoan designers, artists and builders often equalled, and in some way bettered, those of the more ancient civilization of Egypt which was also flourishing at the same period.

Although not generally considered to be one of the

megalithic cultures of Europe, Minoan Crete does, in essence, qualify. It may contain no standing stones or stone circles to parallel those already built and still being constructed in France and far beyond at the time. Nevertheless the Minoans, both on Crete and later on the mainland of Greece, dealt with equally demanding feats of engineering. The so-called "Cyclopean" walls of the Mycenaean stronghold of Mycenae, with their massive stone blocks, were certainly erected by engineers from Crete. The word "megalithic", incidentally, simply means "big stone".

Life further west in the islands of Britain, at a date contemporary with Minoan Crete, was undoubtedly much harder. The Minoans meanwhile came to live a fairly comfortable existence, the political infrastructure of which is not very well understood. Crete at this time may have had a dynastic or an elected monarchy of some sort, though if so it has left no record of having been either overtly authoritarian or repressive. In terms of religion, the chief deity seems to have been a goddess whose personality differed depending on what sphere of life was the focus of attention at any particular point in time. Nature worship was certainly present, with a preference for the depiction on ritual vessels and seals of various types of trees.

It is likely that females, and possibly also males, of a particular class (probably a priesthood) acted out various godly duties as earthly proxies for the deities themselves. Minoan dress, even as depicted in religious settings, is unusual in the extreme. Men are shown wearing little more than a loincloth or a penis sheath whilst the women wore full, flounced skirts below tightly laced bodices that were specifically designed to emphasize bared breasts. Hairstyles were elaborate, as were hats that seem to have served a symbolic or ritual purpose.

Anyone who chooses to study Minoan culture, in so far as it is understood, is soon left with the impression that this was a civilization quite unlike any other that flourished before or since. For example, there is no record anywhere in Crete of a large standing army prior to the incursion of peoples from the

Greek mainland around 1400 BC. It is known that the Minoans had a large merchant navy and that they also possessed a significant number of fighting ships, for it is certain that they dealt with pirates in the Mediterranean and the Aegean from a very early date. However, within the island itself there seems to have been little fear of any sort of civil insurrection. The large palaces, with their vast stores of food and commercial goods for future use or for transhipment, were not fortified and certainly not in a way that could have withstood a determined or hungry mob. This, together with no evidence of a large army, must surely indicate a peaceful populace at ease with life and not anxious to overthrow the status quo, whatever that might have actually been.

Two of the facts that interested us the most with regard to the ancient Minoans (the reasons for which we hope will become obvious as our story unfolds) were their farming techniques and their commercial acumen. We have shown already that Crete is an excellent place for growing a multitude of different crops (in fact probably one of the best in the whole of Europe). One would tend to think, at such an early stage in the rise of human civilizations, that this would merely have fostered a desire within the Minoans to live securely within their own natural sea-washed walls, but this certainly was not the case. From a very early stage in its development, Minoan Crete displayed a desire to take its vast surplus of food produce, together with its manufactured goods such as pottery, and to use it to trade for raw materials in which the island was not rich, for example, copper.

Examples of Minoan merchandise have regularly turned up in various tombs from Egypt. They have been found in the Levant and, though the matter is somewhat contentious, Minoan-type jewellery and goldwork has even been found in the graves of the Wessex Culture, a race living in what is now southern England at a time contemporary with Minoan Crete at its heyday. The Minoans established a chain of outposts throughout the Aegean and the Mediterranean, extending at least as far west as Sicily and probably further still. They traded honey, probably wine, ceramics, jewellery, grain and, in the context of our story the most telling commodity, sheepskins and/or fleece. This trade was probably on a fairly large scale. Soon after the takeover of Crete by the Mycenaeans of mainland Greece sometime around 1400 BC, there are records to indicate that the palace of Knossos alone was running over 50,000 sheep. Bearing in mind that there were at least four other palaces and that private commercial enterprise seems to have been endemic to Minoan civilization, the actual number of sheep being reared on the island must have been colossal.

This early association of very intensive sheep-rearing, allied to a fondness for commercial enterprise and a good head for business and economics, interests us greatly. Of course, even at this early date there is nothing particularly special about rearing sheep, it was going on all over the region, but it is impossible to show examples of such intensity in husbandry from the same period, even in the case of Egypt itself.

We also came to recognize another aspect of Minoan life and society that was to have a profound effect on our studies into much more recent history (though this is inextricably linked to the massive amount of exports leaving Crete during the Minoan era), namely the fact that it seems to have possessed a thriving merchant class. This may not seem too surprising when viewed through modern eyes but commerce, in the accepted sense of the word, was quite unknown in the ancient world. During the Minoan era it was common for one dynastic ruler, say the Pharaoh of Egypt, to receive tribute from another ruler or a client people. Doubtless gifts of the same sort passed in the other direction. Some historians have seen in this habit of "offering gifts" the origins of "trade" in the accepted sense of the word as it would eventually develop.

However, in Minoan Crete it appears that things were rather different. We know that the palaces were rich and vibrant places and that they contained vast storehouses where food and goods for both home consumption and for export were probably stored. One could therefore be forgiven for assuming that tribute, paid by the lower classes to the ruling elite, formed the bulk of the Minoan exports. In all probability such an assumption would be erroneous.

The museum of Heraklion, situated in the capital of modern Crete and close to the ruined palace of Knossos, contains a vast collection of seals. Carved in various forms of stone or very hard wood, the seals seem to have been used as ways of marking merchandise in a way that made it traceable to a particular point of origin. So, for example, a wine vessel would probably be marked with a particular seal at the time of its manufacture to designate, as a French chateau might today, that the liquid in the bottle came from a particular location. It might be presumptive to call these points of origin "companies" in the accepted sense of the word, but there is much on Crete from Minoan times to show the existence of a flourishing middle class which may have been partly made up of private merchants. Plush villas have been located, some very close to the many ports of the island, whilst in those places where everyday Minoan life is viewable, such as in the lava-buried settlement on Santorini, it appears that even the common folk of the Minoans lived a very comfortable life.

Whatever situation predominated prior to about 1450 BC, it was about to change rapidly. The arrival of the mainland Greeks ushered in a far more prohibitive period for the Cretans and an absolute knowledge of the true infrastructure of Minoan life has therefore been lost. However, taking the evidence, and applying a little inference, it was probably as follows.

From lowest to highest, citizens of Minoan Crete owed tribute to one or other of the palaces on the island, though in fact it is likely that the subservient palaces of Phaistos, Malia and Zakro also passed on tribute to Knossos. Why this tribute was paid we cannot know, nor can we be at all certain to whom it was offered (king, queen, priesthood or whatever). Because of the huge proliferation of seals which still exist on Crete (they are often given as presents to brides even today and are known as "milk stones"), it seems likely that almost every member of the society was also in business for his or herself. In so verdant an island as Crete, it would have been quite possible to grow enough crops and rear enough animals to pay a nominal tribute to the ruling class whilst retaining enough for personal consumption and also for export via the merchant class whose job it was to arrange such matters.

There is no evidence of coinage from so early a culture as that of Crete so some sort of "bartering" must have taken place between merchants and peasant farmers, probably farmed and manufactured goods in return for copper or other commodities not readily available in the island. We stress that there is no absolute proof that this was the way Minoan commercial life worked, but the evidence would seem to point in this direction and for one very important reason.

We have already suggested that early archaeologists, such as the Englishman Sir Arthur Evans, were surprised at the lack of protection offered by the palaces against possible civil insurrection. At the same time there is not the slightest evidence that the ruling elite of Minoan Crete possessed a large army. This is in stark contrast to the situation in the Mesopotamian city-states of the period and in Egypt. The inference, therefore, must be that the majority of Minoans were quite content with their lot and this would imply that they had a stake in maintaining a peaceful status quo. This would explain the great number of personal seals from the period that still remain in the island, an indication that practically every Minoan was a trader in his or her own right. In order to fund the sort of life obviously enjoyed by even the lowliest Minoan citizens the economy must have been thriving. Since many of the exported goods were of a perishable nature, for example wool and honey, archaeology can offer only the slimmest clue as to the scale of Minoan exports during the heyday of the civilization. Some decades after the "golden age" of self-determination on Crete, and under Mycenaean domination, Knossos was still running herds of 50,000 sheep so the actual number of sheep, together with cattle and pigs, on the island during the palace period must have been staggering even by modern standards.

It is likely that if the sudden and powerful forces of nature had not lent a hand in the story of the Minoan civilization, it would have gone on to become the single most formative influence in Europe as a whole. In fact it is our intention to show that, despite an overwhelming catastrophe, it probably did in any case. Be that as it may, at some time between 1650 BC and 1450 BC, though most likely around the latter of these two dates, the Minoan civilization as an independent and vibrant self-governing entity ceased to exist. It was at this time that the volcanically unstable island of Thera (also known as Santorini) exploded with an unparalleled ferocity. It probably erupted with a sound louder than any previously heard by humans on this planet and the effects of the cataclysm beggar belief.

Thera is just over 100 kilometres to the north of Crete and the island received the full impact of this cataclysmic occurrence. At least ten times more powerful that the nineteenth-century eruption of Krakatoa, Thera certainly destroyed the infrastructure of Minoan life and probably devastated most cultures immediately to the four compass points of its position. Vast tidal waves followed the eruption, which was really more of a gigantic explosion, and it is likely that, even in a far more sparsely populated Europe than the one we enjoy today, hundreds of thousands of people lost their lives.

Archaeology shows the absolute devastation that followed on Crete, with huge structures literally knocked flat by the force of the initial explosion and by the tidal waves that followed it. In a very short period of time, rule of Crete passed into the hands of the Mycenaean civilization. Much of the very fertile land in the north of the island would have been rendered unusable for at least a decade and it is considered likely that a vast exodus of Cretans took place at this time.

It may or may not be a coincidence that this period matches very neatly a sudden cessation of megalithic building further west. It is a fact that weather patterns changed markedly around the time of the Thera eruption, together with a suspected plague, or series of plagues, that probably decimated populations across the whole body of Europe. There can be no absolute proof that Thera was directly or indirectly responsible for either, but the enforced migration of a large proportion of the Minoan people does seem to have affected many areas surrounding Crete, not least of all the Palestine coast of the Levant. In fact, the very name "Palestine" is directly responsive to Minoan Crete for it derives from the word "Philistine" which is the name given to a particular group of people present in the area by the emerging Hebrews, who themselves were operative in Palestine from about 1400 BC onwards.

Although the impression given of the Philistines by the Old Testament of the Bible indicates a state of almost total conflict with the Hebrews, it is quite likely that a great deal of co-operation and intermarriage took place between the two cultures. There are references to alliances between the Philistines and the Hebrews against their common enemies, the Canaanites. Both the Philistines and the Hebrews were relative newcomers to the region and the Philistines occupied the area around the present Gaza, a location that is referred to time and again in the Old Testament as being Philistine territory.

It is clear that the Hebrews knew the Philistines to be of Cretan origin and doubtless they represented the remnants of the Minoan civilization that had fled from Crete either as a result of the Thera eruption or ahead of the invading Mycenaeans. In the Old Testament we find, in the Book of Amos Chapter 9, verse 7:

Are ye not as children of the Ethiopians unto me, O children of Israel? saith the LORD. Have not I brought up Israel out of the land of Egypt? and the Philistines from Caphtor (Crete), and the Syrians from Kir?

The Prophet Jeremiah also makes the connection for he calls the Philistines "the seashore enemies of the Children of Israel".

The Minoans had certainly been known to the Egyptians too and may, indeed, have run a merchant fleet for them for decades. The Egyptians called the Minoans "the Coifu".

It is interesting to relate that significant amounts of Minoan-type artefacts have been found in Gaza. Latterly the Philistines represented an element of the races referred to by the Egyptians as "the people of the sea". They were greatly feared and appear to have spent several centuries carving out a place for themselves, particularly along the coasts of the Levant. However, at least some elements of Minoan culture found its way well inland and this was particularly the case in Galilee, along the western shore of the Sea of Galilee. There, close to the settlement of Migdal, villas have been excavated that are very Minoan in style. The telltale sign was the discovery of fragments of wall frescos identical to those found in Crete itself, also in the buried and abandoned town of Akoteri, close to the foot of Thera, and in other Minoan settlements.

The Minoans had formed an important part of the "megalithic cultures" originally emanating from the far west of Europe, though thanks to a twist of geological fate, they ultimately found themselves living amidst the Semitic races in the Middle East. This single fact turned out to be extremely important in our search for the origins of both the Cistercian monks and the Templar knights of the Middle Ages. We already knew that there were connections between the happenings of medieval France and Britain and those in Palestine in the last millennium BC, but we had no idea just how very important they would turn out to be.

Chapter 3

The Melting Pot

There is ample evidence to show that the Cistercian order of monks, though founded in France at the beginning of the twelfth century, considered itself to be somehow closely associated with the Levant of Old Testament times. This is particularly the case with regard to Jerusalem at the period of King Solomon, probably around 970 BC. This is also quite evident in the case of the Knights Templar who, to a great extent, were simply an offshoot of the Cistercian order. Doubtless this would be understandable in light of the prevailing Christian beliefs at a period in history when Old Testament studies were of the utmost importance. But what if these people suspected, or even knew of, a more tangible connection with such an early stage in history, other than that brought about by a "partly shared belief system" with the Hebrews?

Our initial research had already shown connections between the families involved in the evolution of the Cistercians and the Templars and the megalithic peoples of Britain and France. Perhaps, we postulated, there were also tangible associations between the same people and the remnants of the Minoan civilization, itself a megalithic culture. At first, the link seemed tentative and unlikely but that situation began to change as our evidence base grew.

The effect of the Minoans, in their alter ego as the Philistines, upon the area of the Levant was probably very significant in the years immediately after the Santorini eruption. The latest evidence shows that groups of fleeing Minoans may have first settled in the Sinai. Doubtless they intermixed with the more or less nomadic tribes living in that area, though with time they seem to have moved up into the Levant itself. It is equally likely that Minoan outposts already existed around Gaza and certainly the archaeological evidence would back up this assertion. In several digs around Gaza significant remains have been unearthed to show a series of Minoan settlements, albeit ones that were heavily influenced by both local and Egyptian customs. This is particularly so in the case of Deir el-Balah and would be very understandable in such a cultural melting pot as the Levant represented at the time. But it is from much further inland that we find the most compelling evidence for the survival of a Minoan way of life that was less altered by local conditions and peoples.

There is one very important location these days, known as Bet-she'an, which is located close to the River Jordan not far south of the Sea of Galilee. Under the accumulated debris of much later periods, a temple was found at Bet-she'an, similar in many ways to those discovered beneath the palace complexes of Minoan Crete. It is known that Bet-she'an was a Philistine location of some importance. It was the place where the Philistines chose to expose the body of King Saul after they, in confederation with the forces of the later Israelite King David, beat Saul and his allies in battle. Despite this alliance, it wasn't long before Bet-she'an fell into Hebrew hands. In later times it became a garrison fort for the Roman occupation of the area, but of its ultimately Minoan foundations there can be no doubt.

As mentioned earlier, a number of obviously Minoan settlements also clung around the western shore of the Sea of Galilee. These share a particular relationship with Bet-she'an in that they occupy a position of 35 degrees 35 minutes east of Greenwich. This longitude conforms absolutely with Xavier

Guichard's longitudinal Salt Line positions. Incredibly, such a line, following the Jordan Valley and running right through the body of the Dead Sea, would seem to be an appropriate longitude to term a "Salt Line" for the Dead Sea is the saltiest place on the Earth. Since we have shown that the Minoans were ultimately of megalithic stock, they would have been aware of the Salt Line system so it is not surprising to us that they chose to place some of their most important settlements in the Levant upon them.

It is possible that Minoan settlements located in Galilee would have fared better under Hebrew domination of the area than other Philistine strongholds further south and west. Even by the era of Jesus Christ, Galilee was not an essentially "Jewish" area. It was peopled by all manner of races with a number of different religious beliefs. There is little evidence that the inhabitants of this region were ever persecuted by the Hebrews, either on account of their racial origins or their beliefs. It seems certain that the village that would eventually come to be known as "Migdal", which in itself means "place of the dove", was of Minoan origin and we will have more to say about this in due course.

The evidence would tend to show that the Minoan presence in the Levant was not a spasmodic affair. On the contrary, the Philistines often represented a serious threat to the emerging Hebrew nation and they are mentioned repeatedly in the Old Testament of the Bible, often oppressing and defeating the Hebrews for decades at a time. However, the reign of King David, probably around 1000 BC, saw the end of the Philistines as an entity that could prove to be a threat to the Israelites, though this may have been as much a response to acceptance and interbreeding as it was to outright subjugation.

We can see from accounts left to us by the chroniclers of the Old Testament that the Philistines were predominantly responsive to a deity whom the Hebrews called "Baal". Baal is a god with a truly ancient pedigree and an oft-mentioned aspect of this religion was bull worship. Alan has shown repeatedly in *The*

Bronze Age Computer Disc just how important bull reverence or worship also was to the Minoans. It is likely that the same was originally true in the case of the Hebrews for at the time of the Exodus from Egypt the Old Testament shows how very difficult it was for Moses to turn his people away from the natural tendency to indulge in bovine worship. Whilst Moses was away from the camps of his people, on Mount Sinai, they started to create "golden calves" around which they were practising religious ceremonies at the time of his return.

If, as we suggest, the Philistines were to have a profound effect on the emerging Hebrews, it would be necessary to show that similar patterns of belief existed between the two peoples. In the past this has always seemed to be unlikely, mainly because the Jews ultimately opted for the severest form of monotheism. The Philistines, as remnants of Minoan civilization in addition to their adoration for the bull, are likely to have accepted a "dual deity" in which male and female components would have played a more or less equal part. It would seem at first sight that this would have been absolutely opposed to a Jewish view of deity, though this impression is misleading.

We began to investigate the early belief patterns of the Philistines and discovered that they did indeed have a reverence for the feminine. In reality, the Philistines and associated peoples have left us notice of many gods and goddesses among the peoples of the Levant. For example, the Hebrews adopted Dagon, the mermaid-like goddess of the Philistines, and one that would seem to represent the beliefs of a seafaring people such as the Minoans.

Dagon, in a similar fashion to the goddess Derceto of the Syrians, had the body of a beautiful and powerful woman ending in a large tail of a fish. We could not help but draw our minds to the legend of Merovinus, the first king of the Merovingian dynasty, which we will look at in detail in another chapter of this book. Legend has it that Merovinus was born of human and sea monster. We wondered if perhaps this legend dated back to a Minoan origin.

Even with the present research at hand, the popular conception is that the Hebrews were the world's first monotheists. It is an opinion that we believe to be in error, as clearly the Egyptian Amenhotep IV and the Zoroastrians predate the Hebrew monotheistic belief by some time.

Our main window on Hebrew history is the Old Testament of the Bible. This is a confusing document but it does seem to have the ring of historical authenticity about it and, indeed, in some respects this is the case. But we should not be too willing to accept everything the Old Testament has to tell us with regard to the early history of the Israelites, and for one very important reason. The Old Testament as we know it today, though carrying a wealth of race memories and oral traditions, was not written at the times that its various events took place. In fact, it is fairly easy to ascertain when the various Books that comprise the earliest part of the Old Testament were first committed to writing, on account of their content. In around 590 BC Israel was beaten in battle by the forces of Babylon and many of the Hebrews were taken to Babylon as captives. It was during this period of exile that something akin to modern Judaism was born. There, the disparate traditions of a number of more or less affiliated tribes were welded into a common, though often inaccurate, history.

The Babylonian origins of the Old Testament are apparent for a number of reasons. For example, some of the oldest stories of the Bible, those relating to the Creation, to the Garden of Eden and particularly to the Flood, are of Babylonian origin. Similar accounts of a much earlier date have been found written on clay tablets in the area. So to use the Old Testament as the basis for establishing the truth underpinning the earliest days of the Hebrews would be dubious to say the least.

It was very important, whilst in Babylon, for the Israelites to concoct a cohesive view of Judaism, which is presumably why a "unique identity" was fabricated at that time, in reality many centuries after the lives and events that lay beneath the narrative. When we also bear in mind that the accounts of kings such as Solomon retain distinctly un-Jewish components, which doubtless slipped by the careful pens of the new Jewish chroniclers, we begin to realize that ancient history for the Hebrew peoples may have been substantially different than the Bible would lead us to believe.

The early Hebrews were probably not half so inclined to monotheism as seems to be the case. In fact there is strong circumstantial evidence that this was not true at all. It is a peculiarity of the early Israelites that they considered their god (although presumably also "omnipresent") to reside in the sacred box that they called the "Ark of the Covenant". It sounds ludicrous in modern terms to think of God living in a box, but there really isn't any doubt that this is what the Israelite priests believed. After the founding of Jerusalem and the building of the Temple, the Ark resided in a special section of the Temple known as the "Holy of Holies". Only a certain section of the priesthood was allowed into this room and even then only once a year, after many ritualistic cleansings.

It was in this sacred space that the earliest Jews believed that the sacred "communion" between God and Goddess took place. Here between the golden wings of the cherubim, God would sit. This spot known as the "Mercy Seat" was the throne of God during his communion with the priest. After the defeat of the Israelites by the Babylonian forces of Nebuchadnezzar, the Ark was lost, as indeed was the Temple for quite some time. Since it was only in the Ark of the Covenant, and specifically in Jerusalem, that the conjoining of God and Goddess could take place, it was considered that the female side of the partnership had been lost and that the Goddess would henceforth roam the world.

It should also be remembered that the Jews had fought tenaciously for every scrap of land they eventually inhabited in the Levant. Our extensive review of ancient history has led us to a specific belief regarding views of a "balanced" deity in which the female component retains its importance. It seems to us that the more martial and warlike a culture is forced into being, usually by circumstances, the more it tends to lean in the direction of the "masculine" aspect of godhead. The enforced slavery of the children of Israel in Babylon seems to have added to entrenched values a sense of extreme nationalism and a search for both homeland and identity. Under such conditions it is probably not at all surprising that the Jews ultimately opted for a "Father God" who they assumed would finally lead them to victory in battle.

In short, we should certainly not run away with the idea that just because modern Judaism fails to respond to any tangible "feminine" quality within the godhead, that this has always been the case. On the contrary, in Jewish folk stories, if not actually in the Bible itself, there is specific mention of Adam's first wife (and probably a vestige of the former Goddess) who is referred to as "Lilith".

According to these legends, Lilith was formed at the same time as Adam from the same material and was therefore, to her mind, his equal. In some traditions the two started out as one androgynous being, united physically. In either case, so the tale goes, a dispute arose over the position for sexual coupling. Lilith, from her standpoint of being Adam's equal, objected to his request for her to lie beneath him and, in protest to his requests for male superiority, spoke the ineffable name of God. In answer to the call she immediately sprouted wings and took flight, escaping from the garden that would surely be her imprisonment. Three angels were dispatched to capture and return her to the Garden of Eden. Rather than face a life as a man's slave, she threw herself into the Red Sea. From this time on Lilith has been a representation of the female right of equality and rebellion.

We should point out briefly at this point that modern Judaism does retain one female religious association in the form of the "Shakinah", or Bride of God, who is a major aspect of sabbath celebrations. Jewish song tells of the coming of the Shakinah on the sabbath and compares the holy day to the Bride of God. So in this respect, there resides within modern Judaism an aspect of female divinity within the godhead.

The Bible is the main window of Jewish history of a very early date. However, the Bible was so radically altered when first committed to the written word, it is now difficult to be absolutely sure about what mainstream Israelite belief may have been when these nomadic tribes began carving out a state for themselves west of the Jordan. But it is also plain to see that the first Bible chroniclers failed to eradicate all traces of pre-Jewish material from what had originally been an oral tradition. To show this, we need look no further than biblical accounts of King Solomon who is, after all, an extremely important character when viewed through the eyes of specific groups. Amongst these groups are the Cistercians and the Templars of medieval France and even the Freemasons of today. King Solomon has the reputation of being a truly "wise" king and who is venerated above all Jewish monarchs with the possible exception of David. But it terms of "Jewishness" in the modern sense of the word, there appears to be no justification for this. It is quite plain from biblical accounts that Solomon would have little in common with the Jewish community of the modern age.

As an example, monogamy is enshrined in modern Judaism and supposedly has been from the very start. However, this cannot always have been the case because the Book of Kings tells us that Solomon had: "seven hundred wives, princesses, and three hundred concubines". One of these wives was an Egyptian princess, the daughter of the Pharaoh, for whom Solomon built a palace immediately adjacent to the Temple on the most holy site in Jerusalem.

Solomon didn't always content himself with service to the God of the Israelites, for the Book of Kings goes on to suggest that Solomon "went after Ashtoreth, the goddess of the Zidonians, and after Milcom the abomination of the Ammonites". Even those agencies that Solomon employed in the construction of the Temple to YHWH (Yahveh) were not of monotheistic beliefs. The majority of the workmen came from Tyre which at that time was a centre of goddess worship.

Clearly the Old Testament writers of the Babylonian era,

writing centuries after these events, were not happy with
Solomon's behaviour. In fact the biblical passages in question
are couched in terms that make it plain that some of the ultimate
privations of Israel were, latterly, blamed on Solomon's
behaviour. But this is a view entirely attributable to a later and
very different religious and social need. In other words, it has
been funded by sanctimonious hindsight. It is made clear time
and again that the Jews of the period of Solomon were almost
entirely different from those following the much later
Rabbinical Judaism of the present age.

As further proof of King Solomon's respect for, and even
adoration of, the Goddess as well as God, we would wish to refer
the reader to a strange little book of the Old Testament known as
"Solomon's Song of Songs". The authors Lynn Picknett and
Clive Prince, in their book *The Templar Revelation,* showed
conclusively that the Song of Songs conforms very closely to a
wedding rite of Egyptian and specifically Isis-based religious
worship. That such a book should still be present in a Bible
penned by Jewish scholars is little short of incredible. The whole
narrative of the Song of Songs is shot through with orgiastic
symbolism of a type much more commonly associated with the
ancient "mystery religions", all of which responded either specifically to goddess worship or to a paired deity, such as Isis and
Osiris, and Demeter and Dionysus.

In passing, we would like to draw the reader's attention to the
fact that the Song of Songs was of particular fascination to St
Bernard of Clairvaux, the true father of the Cistercian and
Templar orders. Bernard wrote literally dozens of sermons on
the Song of Songs. This is a theme to which we shall return in
due course.

Solomon was a tough, practical man, living as king over a
group of people who had only recently become urbanized. For
centuries, the tribes that would eventually become Israel had
been wandering up and down the Jordan, finding grazing for
their livestock and seeking the best life they could for
themselves amongst the warring factions of the area. The great

nation these people ultimately became is not in doubt, though what they represented in religious terms during the reign of King Solomon, and for centuries after, is almost certainly radically different than later Bible chroniclers either realized or would have been willing to admit. The distinguished researcher and author B.S.J. Isserlin, in his book *The Israelites*, is at pains to point out that amongst deities undoubtedly worshipped by the earlier, pre-exile Israelites was the Canaanite goddess Asherah. This deity is much akin to the old neolithic "Earth Mother" whose worship seems to have been perpetuated in Crete from the very beginning of the Minoan civilization. Also of Canaanite origin was Baal (the name also given by the Bible scribes to the god of the Philistines). In the Canaanite context Baal was the son or grandson of El, the chief god of the Canaanite pantheon. Isserlin sees in Baal, which means "Master" or "Lord", an annually dying and rising god. This could be particularly relevant and is a theme that will resurface when we come to discus the "secret" beliefs of both the Cistercians and the Knights Templar.

Ezekiel, writing in the sixth century BC, tells of Israel's worship of Tammuz, the young lover of Ishtar (the mother goddess). According to myth, when Tammuz dies and descends to the nether world he is followed by Ishtar who attempts to rescue him from the powers that hold him. Whilst away, all vegetation dies and the world remains barren until the couple returns to the surface at which time nature celebrates and the crops grow once again. This is so close to the story of Demeter and Persephone, from later Greek cycles, that there must surely be a connection. By common consent, Demeter and Persephone are ultimately of Cretan origin.

Also of relevance to the early Israelites were various Phoenician deities, particularly the goddess Ashtarte, together with the gods and goddesses of other people with whom they came into contact in the Levant. Isserlin is fairly silent with regard to specific Philistine influences within early Israelite religion, but any lack of absolute evidence with this regard may be due to the propensity of the first biblical scribes for lumping certain deities together under specifically Hebrew names, such as in the case of Baal. It becomes impossible, therefore, to know with any certainty whether the scribes in any particular passage are referring to a Phoenician deity, a Canaanite god or a Philistine one unless the text makes the matter plain. In any case, it is not our intention to try and prove that early Israelite religion was specifically responsive to the Philistine/Minoan connection. We merely wish to show that it added to the religious melting pot of the region during the late Bronze Age and early Iron Age.

Regarding Philistine influence during this crucial period of the founding of Jerusalem we do recognize patterns that could be significant. It seems that many of the numbering systems that were endemic to the megalithic peoples of Crete and the far west of Europe are also attributable to Jewish sources at the time of Solomon. These would cease to be important, except in a purely symbolic sense, with the passing of time. Initially, however, their use in conjunction with the period of Solomon seems to indicate some survival of megalithic knowledge in the Palestine of the period. The Book of Kings states that the Temple of Solomon was built exactly 480 years after the Exodus. This is one of the most telling time periods mentioned in the Old Testament and is almost certain to be Philistine and ultimately Minoan in origin. It is a deeply sacred megalithic number because megalithic cycles were of 40 years, and 480 years is simply 40 multiplied by 12. But this is not the end of the story. If the 366-day calendar of the megalithic peoples was not subject to the alterations indicated by the second, 123-day calendar, they would eventually rectify themselves after 480 ritual years. The simple reason for this fact is that 480 years of 366 days is the same as 481 solar years of 365.25 days (or at any rate incredibly close). So, what the Bible is saying here is that the period of time between the Exodus and the building of the Jerusalem Temple was of one full, great megalithic cycle. This period is of no significance whatsoever in lunar terms, and orthodox Jewish calendar practices were entirely lunar-based.

The 480-year round is a totally "solar" phenomenon and more closely matches some of the calendar principles of the Essene, about whom we will have more to say in due course.

The internal dimensions of Solomon's Temple, as outlined in the Book of Kings, shows an interior area of 360,000 cubic cubits, which is an astronomically based, solar-derived number. The Bible tells us that the Temple was built with Phoenician assistance, though once again this would demonstrate that the early Israelites were open to all manner of cultural influences as their own, eventually rich culture was in an evolutionary stage.

Isserlin also points out the importance of the first Israelites to the "High Places" which were hilltop shrines regularly mentioned in the Old Testament. Where archaeological excavations have taken place in such sites, there seems to be another striking parallel with known Minoan religious practices. Greek archaeologists have found many examples of hill and mountaintop shrines of a similar sort in Crete. In addition, tree worship of a sort also recognized in Minoan Crete seems to have been practised in many parts of the Israeli-controlled Levant.

Away from purely religious matters, we should perhaps take a look at an aspect of Minoan life that also became important to the Hebrews in the Levant, namely the rearing of sheep and goats. Of course the ancestors of the Hebrews were nomadic tribes whose very lives depended on livestock of this sort. In fact this had probably been the case from a period long before Minoan Crete rose from the neolithic twilight to become a recognizable civilization. However, by the time a "Jewish State" had been carved out in the Levant, the husbandry of sheep seems to have reached gigantic proportions. With this regard, it is not beyond the realms of possibility that the great acumen of Minoan (latterly Philistine) farmers played a part in the story.

Isserlin, using well-accepted estimations, considers that by the seventh century BC the number of sheep within Israelite-controlled areas was between 600,000 and 700,000, though this number would also include goats. When this is set against estimates of 800,000 sheep and goats from the same geographical area for a date as recent as 1923, a sensible comparison can be made. If this comparatively up-to-date estimation is adjusted to account for trans-Jordan flocks, which have been included in the Iron Age calculations, the numbers are not all that dissimilar. However, it is quite likely that the Iron Age Levant actually had more livestock of this sort than can be found in the area today.

Wool was of tremendous importance to the Hebrews and formed the most commonly used textiles for the populace as a whole. Whether the Israelites, as we know to have been the case with the Minoans, were producing a surplus of wool for export cannot be reliably ascertained. However, it is quite possible that Minoan farming methods, via the Philistines, led the Hebrews to use a type of sheep more suited to a more settled form of existence than that experienced by their nomadic ancestors.

In summary, we know that a large number of Minoans escaping from the ravages of the Santorini eruption ultimately found their way to Levant. There, they became the Philistines of biblical fame and, in their association with the Hebrews, they undoubtedly contributed in great part to the evolution of modern Judaism. We know that they frequented Salt Lines in both Gaza and the Jordan Valley and that they contributed solar calendar-inspired practices and numbers to a generally lunar-based, Semitic-type religion. It is clear that they had a definite impact on a culture that was to emerge as a power in its own right and it is for this reason that their original importance has been marginalized by later Hebrew writers. However, it is clear that the Hebrews became an entity entirely because of the inter-racial mixing of nomadic Semitic tribes and other peoples they encountered in the Levant. One of the peoples with whom they lived and fought the most was the Philistines.

We now need to try and discover if any peculiarly Minoan, and therefore megalithic, influences were retained within Jewish society to surface at a later and probably more crucial date.

Chapter 4

The Dead Sea Community

In the year 1947, a young Arab shepherd boy accidentally stumbled across one of the most important historical treasures ever brought to light. He was wandering with his flocks amidst rock faces and isolated caves northwest of the Dead Sea, near a place called Qumran, when he happened upon remote caves which contained significant numbers of scrolls. What he discovered has since caused a sensation amongst biblical scholars. The original find may not have been considered all that important, but it didn't take long for experts to flock to the location. There they found a whole series of ancient pots which contained scrolls and fragments of scrolls that were obviously of a great age.

As more and more discoveries were made in other caves, most of which were close to the first, it became obvious that here was a hidden library, almost certainly secreted away in the months leading up to the fateful time in AD 70 when the Roman army under Vespasian, stung by a Jewish revolt in Jerusalem, raced through the Jordan Valley destroying everything of Hebrew origin that lay in its path. The Jews had been under the heel of the Romans for some time prior to this revolt and had always been more or less unwilling servants of the Roman Empire. Finally, edicts relating to the Jewish unwillingness to recognize Roman divinities, together with a host of less religious and more practical problems, led to a bitter and bloody war which resulted in the total destruction of self-determining Judea. The various scrolls found at Qumran and in other locations represented much of the written material that would have been held as sacred or politically important to the leaders of the Jews immediately prior to the uprising and it is obvious that they had been secreted in the caves in the knowledge that a catastrophe was looming. Included amongst the fragments were copies of every book of the Old Testament, except for Esther, some of which were represented time and again in different forms.

What surprised experts most was the wealth of additional material that came to light. Much of this seemed to relate to an otherwise little understood Jewish or quasi-Jewish sect known as the Essene. Something was known of this sect of heretical Jews from earlier sources but the Qumran discoveries filled in much of the missing detail. Close by the Qumran caves archaeologists discovered the ruins of a curious little settlement which carbon dating showed to be contemporary with the hiding of Dead Sea Scrolls, the name by which the accumulated documents had come to be known. More and more careful sifting of the finds at Qumran led the experts to believe that what had once occupied the site was a sort of early pre-Christian monastery. Material contained in many of the documents discovered nearby showed that the whole library of information to be found in the caves may easily have been secreted there by the people inhabiting the settlement of Qumran immediately prior to the Jewish uprising.

It is now believed that the Essene may have existed as a sect within Judaism from about 200 BC, though how much they had altered during the almost three centuries of their existence will probably never be known. They seem to have formed isolated communities, mainly composed of men, and they considered themselves to be a sort of chosen elect within Judaism, to whom the final redemption of Jewish society would be vouchsafed.

The Essene were staunch upholders of Jewish law, but they appear to have also adhered to a number of rules, regulations and religious practices that were less than typical of Judaism as a whole. Essene belief revolved around an individual they called the "Teacher of Righteousness". It is not known for certain who this individual may have been but a prime candidate, and one cited by many experts, is James the Just. James figures prominently in the life and ministry of Jesus Christ. Some authorities consider him to have been the brother of Jesus because in the New Testament he referred to himself in these terms. However it is quite possible that he used the word "brother" in a figurative rather than a literal sense.

Despite uncertainty regarding the relationship between James and Jesus, there seems to be as much hard evidence relating to the existence of James the Just as there is for Jesus himself. In other words, there is no doubt of his historical existence as a character of some religious influence in the early decades of the modern era. If James is to be recognized as the "Teacher of Righteousness" of Essene fame, then the oft-mooted theory that Jesus was ultimately a disciple of Essene teaching might be substantiated. There are similarities between the ideas put forward by both John the Baptist and Jesus, and those of the Essene, though some experts also recognize a dissimilar approach to certain spiritual and Jewish law imperatives that make the association less likely. What is equally possible, however, is that later insertions in the corpus of information contained in the New Testament tend to sway the teachings of John and Jesus away from their original intentions.

The Essene kept strict laws of conduct and were, in almost every respect, an institution that would be paralleled by medieval monasticism of the most austere sort. Certainly the Essene broke away from the status quo of the day to seek a more strict form of observance. We know that the Essene wore white robes, that they kept all property in common and that they renounced the outside world. All of their communities appear to have been stretched out along the western shores of the Jordan and the Dead Sea where they had gone to great trouble to ensure a clean and constant water supply. The Essene had created large water cisterns and had extremely strict rules about the supply and usage of "latrines" at some distance from their settlement. These measures infer a close attention to particular rules about cleanliness and hygiene. It is also highly likely that the Essene kept large flocks of sheep.

It is quite possible that the Essene were not originally of Jewish origin. They adhered to a solar calendar rather than the more common Semitic lunar calendar of the Hebrews themselves. (In this respect, at least, they could have had much in common with the ex-Minoan Philistines) Some of the written evidence indicates that they believed in a sort of Pythagorean "reincarnation" or "transmigration of souls" after death and they adhered to many rules and regulations that would have seemed perplexing or even absurd to mainstream Jews of their own day. Despite these differences, it is obvious that the Essene believed Judaism to be out of step with their own beliefs and not the other way round.

It is interesting to note that not one but in fact several of the ruins that are thought to have been of ultimately Essene creation are located in the immediate vicinity of the longitudinal Salt Line that follows the Jordan Valley. In the case of Qumran, where this line passes through the Dead Sea itself, the community is as near to the longitudinal Salt Line as the need for a water supply and shelter allows it to be.

It is highly likely that the Essene were somehow associated with groups such as the Zealots. The Zealots were a paramilitary body dedicated to throwing the Romans out of the area altogether, and it was groups such as this whose actions sealed the fate of the region at the time of the uprising in AD 70. The Essene, whilst generally dedicated to a life of seclusion, left documents that indicated their readiness to associate themselves with the overthrow of the Romans and they even planned military strategies for the final battle that must have seemed imminent in the years leading up to AD 70.

One document in particular, called the "War Rule Scroll", was found in 1951 in cave number one. It consists of nineteen badly damaged columns of parchment and is therefore one of the least complete of the scrolls found at Qumran. It represents a rather important aspect of Dead Sea Scroll research as it reflects Essene thought regarding the expected end of the world. It would also seem to suggest the presence of an Essene military force or, at the very least, a planned one. Whether this intended army was to defend the Essene against the hordes of hell or merely the coming Roman troops, we cannot know for sure, but nonetheless the documents exist. Column five discusses the disposition and weapons of the front formations while column six discusses the movements of the attacking infantry and the disposition and movements of the cavalry, which would indicate mounted soldiers or at least the plans for such a body.

According to column five, which deals with the weapons to be used, it can be seen that each type was to be of a specific length, width and particularly ornate design. The swords were to be made from pure iron and refined in such a way as to look like a mirror. Both sides of the blade were to contain the image of ears of corn pointing towards the sword's tip. The length of each sword was to be 1.5 cubits with a blade width of 4 fingers. Real or speculative, there can be no doubt that the Essene intended their army to take part in a "Holy War".

Specific patterns of advancement are outlined in column six which tells us that three divisions of foot soldiers shall arrange themselves and that the first flank shall hurl seven javelins towards the enemy formations. On the javelins were to be written religious phrases such as "Bloody spikes to bring down the slain by the wrath of God", further evidence of an army prepared not merely for battle, but for spiritual warfare of the most elevated kind.

Whether or not the Essene actually maintained their own military wing is not known, but it is a fact that Qumran and all the other supposed Essene communities were destroyed as the armies of Vespasian swept through the area.

What must now be taken as certain is that the Essene, though seekers of desert seclusion, maintained good relations with certain agencies within Jerusalem itself. One of the documents found in the Qumran hoard was a copper scroll that itemized the nature and hiding places of Temple furniture and documents secreted beneath the Temple Mount in Jerusalem. It is hard to explain how the Essene could have been party to such information if they had not had a hand in planning it.

It is possible that astronomical and astrological ideas played a part in Essene belief. Found in cave number four were two documents dating, according to scholars, from the first century BC. The first, in Hebrew, and the second, in Aramaic, involve a connection between an individual's features, his destiny and the configuration of the stars at the time of his birth.

Much of the Essene ceremony and the information left to us relates to a character known as the "Lord of Light". An alternative name for a very similar character in ancient times was "Lucifer". This latter name has tended to attach itself to the Devil, but Lucifer actually means "Lord of Light" and once specifically related to the planet Venus when viewed as an evening star. Essene belief was of a partly apocalyptical nature, and seems to have much in common with the sort of sentiments expressed in the Book of Revelations. Above all, the Essene believed themselves to be the "chosen" amongst Jewish sects and the rightful legatees of the "New Jerusalem" that would be established, as indicated in the War Rule found at Qumran, when the enemies (presumably the Romans) were defeated. The Essene maintained a Spartan and ascetic existence and appear to have contributed, in part at least, to the messianic prophecies that were so rife in their region around the time of Jesus.

The Essene seems to have had an important part to play in a particular area of early Christianity, namely monasticism. The sort of life that they led, their aspirations and their desire for seclusion has much in common with the most ascetic forms of Christian monasticism, some of which sprang up within a couple of hundred years of the ministry of Jesus. However, despite the attempts of the "Desert Fathers" of Egypt, people such as St Anthony the Hermit, Simon Stylites and others, the closest parallels we can discover to the Essene in almost every way did not arise until about a full thousand years after their time. The severest form of Benedictine monasticism only approaches that of the communities of the Essene and we can find no monastic institution anywhere near as similar to the Essene communities as that of the much later Cistercians. Despite the disparity regarding time-scale and geographical location, it is worth itemizing some of these similarities:

- The Essene specifically chose remote desert locations for their settlements, so did the Cistercians, for the word "desert" is specifically mentioned in the Order of the Cistercians. Both groups deliberately sought seclusion and redemption through both work and prayer.
- Both brotherhoods wore white. It isn't known if the Essene placed the same reliance on sheep-rearing as did the Cistercians, but the likelihood is that they did and their garments, like those of the Cistercians, were undoubtedly of non-dyed and possibly bleached wool.
- Cistercians and Essene alike showed a great obsession with cleanliness and sanitary living conditions. This was not an exclusive consideration of all monastic settlements by any stretch of the imagination. The Essene may or may not have practised total immersion as a form of repeated baptism. There is no written evidence that this was the case and the cisterns found at Qumran and other locations may merely have been a means of retaining water in an extremely arid area. The Cistercians were expected to wash their heads, hands and arms daily. This might seem a perfunctory accession to cleanliness when seen from our modern perspective, but in medieval terms it was viewed with surprise and even alarm by some agencies. Like the Essene, the Cistercians made superhuman efforts to supply all parts of their monasteries and other establishments with ample water for all

manner of uses. The layout of a typical Cistercian abbey might incorporate a modified stream, as at Fountains Abbey in Yorkshire, England, as well as waste water channels and other indications of an ingenious effort to supply every part of the establishment with running water. Similar efforts were made at Qumran as well as at the Minoan palace of Knossos, where the supply of fresh water to all parts of the building was broadly similar, as were the precautions taken for drainage and the disposal of sewage. We dare to suggest the Minoan/Philistine know-how, amassed over many centuries, might easily have been employed in the planning and building of settlements such as Qumran.

- Essene and Cistercians alike maintained a belief in the founding of a "New Jerusalem". If we are to believe that the Essene "Teacher of Righteousness" was indeed James the Just, then we can also recognize the emergence of a common belief pattern. James never seems to have considered either Jesus or himself to be the founders of a new religion so much as a progressed form of Judaism. This fact introduces us to evidence relating to the early Cistercians as a whole and to St Bernard of Clairvaux in particular. At a time when Jews were continually being persecuted in western Europe, St Bernard went to great lengths to support their communities, even when to do so may have gone against his own best interests. On several occasions, he travelled great distances to put down pogroms, and he maintained a number of Jewish scribes and scholars within the confines of his own abbey of Clairvaux. He was also a staunch supporter of the Jewish Cabalistic schools that flourished in cities such as Troyes and Rouen.

- By their very nature both the Essene doctrine and that of the Cistercians harked back to the dawn of Judaism and the founding of the First Temple by Solomon. It should be remembered that the Templars were actually named after this institution (the Poor Soldiers of Christ and the Temple of Solomon). This is largely due to the fact that they, as did many Christian Crusaders, believed the al-Aqsa Mosque on the Temple Mount to have been Solomon's Temple, a place of particular importance and reverence to the Templar knights. Time and again, St Bernard returned to the life of Solomon in his sermons and in particular to Solomon's Song of Songs. The fascination that both the Cistercians and the Templars held for this early period of Jewish history is quite without parallel and set the standard for the Old Testament interest prevailing in Europe at the time.

- Both groups believed that the final battle, preparatory to the creation of the New Jerusalem, would represent a physical as well as a spiritual struggle. As we have seen earlier in this chapter, one of the documents found at Qumran is known as the War Rule Scroll and it details the last and greatest battle that will have to be fought against the forces of darkness. This is not simply a hypothetical document based on spiritual beliefs. On the contrary, it gives very specific military advice and instructions. We have seen how it identifies the form of armaments to be carried, together with the clothing and headgear that should be worn. Beyond this, it specifies a system of signals to be used at times of war. This is a strange document to have been compiled by a body that generally existed to wage a spiritual rather than tangible war against its enemies. Nevertheless, it is more than paralleled in the case of the Cistercians. It should be remembered that the Knights Templar were a wholly Cistercian institution and that the Templar "rule" was merely a modification of that created for the Cistercians themselves. The Templars were dedicated in the name of the most sacred Jewish location imaginable and they too existed to wage war against the forces of darkness as these were recognized during their period.

The more we looked at all these similarities, the more diffi-cult they were to dismiss, but they also seemed rather dubious, particularly since there was a gap of ten centuries separating the Essene and the Cistercians. Of course we are not the first researchers by any means to suggest that there might be a connection between the Jewish monasticism of the Essene and early Christian monastic institutions. In fact it would be unlikely that such a connection could possibly be dismissed. Although the consideration of these associations is compelling our hypothesis goes far beyond this. We would go so far as to suggest that there was an awareness on the part of the founders of Cistercianism of the existence of the Essene, their motives, organization and the structure of their religious settlements. We hope to demonstrate how such an unlikely scenario could have been brought about. Before we can do this, it is first necessary to learn a little more about the political and religious climate during which the Essene flourished, and about St James the Just who was their probable "Teacher of Righteousness".

Whether or not James actually was the brother of Jesus, we shall probably never know. At least part of the reason for believing that he may have been the Essene "Teacher of Righteousness" lies in the fact that James is often referred to as "James the Righteous". He appears to have acquired this name as a result of his behaviour which was always directly in accordance with Jewish law. According to the second-century Christian historian Hegesippus, James always wore priestly clothes and was allowed to enter the inner sanctum of the Temple, which would only have been possible for a high-ranking priest. James believed that Christianity was a natural outcome of Judaism and it is unlikely that he would ever have envisaged the belief as being remotely interesting to non-Jews. Most orthodox Jews generally saw no problem in the teaching of James and it was, in the main, the high Jewish authorities, the chief priests and officials, who thought him dangerous. The Sadducees, in particular, sought his downfall and it was they, history relates, who threw him from a high parapet close to the Temple sometime around AD 66. Essene teaching seemed to imply that the "Teacher of Righteousness" had met a violent death and this fact bolsters the belief that the "Teacher of Righteousness" and James the Just may have been one and the same person.

Perhaps the murder of James was one of the factors that spurred the commencement of the Jewish uprising because it was in the same year that the high priests of the Temple were killed by Zealot sympathizers, who accused them of being lackeys of the Roman administration. Soon after this, the Roman garrison was driven from Jerusalem, and a few years later the Jews received the most fatal blow that was ever meted out to such an unfortunate people until more modern times.

So it can be seen that the battle was chiefly against Roman occupation and Roman tyranny. This is a fact that our ultimate evidence forced us to bear in mind, for there are parallels between the Essene and Zealot view of Roman rule and the view that the early Cistercians seem to have had of the ruling Roman Catholic Church of their day. These parallels should become ever more evident as our story unfolds. We must also bear in mind that James the Just was, during his lifetime, the undisputed head of the Christian Church in Jerusalem. This title fell to him after the arrest of Paul and the flight of Peter to Rome. Actually, we have no way of knowing if St Peter did travel to the capital of the Empire for there is only legend to assert that this was the case. As far as St Paul is concerned, there is much evidence to indicate that he and James the Just were not on good terms. Doubtless Paul of Tarsus, had he still been living at the time, would have shed few, if any, tears over the martyrdom of a man who threatened his hold over the emerging religion. James, after all, never saw Christianity as anything of the sort and does not appear to have sought Gentile converts, as was clearly the case with Paul.

Above all, it seems self-evident that one of the most important considerations of the Essene was to free Jerusalem from the hands of people considered to be tyrants. In terms of the period in question, this can only have alluded to the forces of Rome and that section of Jewish society that supported their rule. Only with the removal of the legions, and with chosen priests replacing Roman puppets in the Temple, could Israel live again as the religious and political entity that Solomon had created so many centuries previously. It is a little known fact that the agencies so instrumental in urging the First Crusade against the Holy Land in the latter part of the eleventh century had exactly the same motivation, and though they couldn't express it volubly, they also fostered the same hatred of Rome as did the Essene. Chief amongst these people were the Cistercians and their military wing, the Knights Templar.

Chapter 5

The Hidden Years

It is impossible to say what happened to the brotherhood of the Essene after the Jewish uprising in AD 70. Doubtless the majority of them were slaughtered, as were so many Jewish citizens at the time. This fate is even more likely if the fraternity was considered to be allied to the Zealot cause. It does seem likely, however, that some of them escaped. Had they done so, it would have been sensible for them to travel to places on the fringe, or even beyond the borders, of the Roman Empire. Even prior to this period Jews had become inveterate travellers and traders, and were to be found spread across the length and breadth of the known world.

Essene survivors may or may not have been supporters of the Christian cause. In fact, if James the Just really can be taken to represent the Essene "Teacher of Righteousness", then it is virtually certain that they would have at least paid lip-service to some form of Christianity. But since to them, as well as to James himself, this form of Christianity was nothing more than an "improvement" of mainstream Judaism, its rightful location must always be Jerusalem, the religious and administrative centre of Solomon's dream. The truth of Essene and Jamesite Christianity would certainly never be found in Rome and yet, paradoxically, this is exactly where the home of Christianity was to establish itself.

The reasons for this are fairly self-evident. Despite the best efforts of a whole succession of Roman emperors, Christianity grew and prospered. No sooner had one community been rooted out somewhere in the Roman world than another one appeared and began to flourish. In fact the Roman authorities had no real argument with people wishing to be Christians. The Roman Empire was probably the most religiously tolerant administration in history because it really didn't care what its citizens believed, but it did take a great interest in what they did. The main complaint regarding Christians was that they refused to accept the overall supremacy (and at some stages the supposed divinity) of the Roman emperors. Christians were also accused of being intolerant of other faiths and of the destruction of the temples belonging to law-abiding Roman citizens.

By the fourth century AD it was becoming obvious that Christianity would never be defeated by persecuting its adherents, a course of action which only served to encourage more and more recruits. By this period the Roman Empire was in serious difficulties on many of its borders. It had become over-extended and badly run, with ever more incursions of "barbarian hordes" stretching its military resources. It was at this crucial time that an emperor emerged who addressed the Christian problem in a new way. This man must have reasoned that Christianity had now become so powerful that within it lay the best interests of the Roman Empire as a whole. It must also have occurred to him that the imposition of a state religion would help to re-cement the crumbling masonry of the Empire. To a great extent his reasoning was sound, and it is to this man, the Emperor Constantine, that we must credit not only the acceptance of Christianity but also its absolute adoption as the future religion of the Roman Empire.

Flavius Valerius Constantinus or, as he would latterly come to be known, Constantine the Great was born on 27 February, probably in the year AD 288, although there is great debate among academics over the exact year. His father, Constantius I Chlorus, was a high-ranking soldier who, despite his position in the Roman army, was not of an aristocratic stock, but rather was the son of a simple goatherd. Constantine's mother was an evocative character of whom we shall learn more in due course. Her name was Helena.

In AD 293 Constantine's father was raised to the rank of Caesar, and his son ultimately succeeded him in the year 306 while both (arguably) were resident in the English garrison city of York. Constantine's accession to the rank of emperor was not unopposed but he eventually gained supremacy over his rivals. Local tradition has it that Helena, Constantine's mother, was none other than a British princess and the daughter of the King Cole of nursery-rhyme fame. Modern historians doubt this interpretation of Helena's origins but there is much circumstantial evidence to suggest that this may indeed have been the case. Constantine was brought up in the rabidly anti-Christian circles of the court of the Emperor Diocletian, though tradition has it that his British mother was a staunch Christian from before the birth of her famous son.

Undoubtedly, Constantine's eventual acceptance of Christianity was spurred on by political rather than religious considerations and it is not even certain that he ever embraced the faith himself. He is much more likely to have been an advocate of a deity known as "Sol Invictus". Constantine was born of a culture that was well at home with a whole cocktail of different deities so it is unlikely that he would have seen any conflict of interests in at least tolerating Christians within the Empire (as long as it suited his own political ends).

There are many legends associated with Constantine's supposed conversion to Christianity but none are as prevalent as the one relating to his victory over Maxentius on the Milvian Bridge in Rome. Having successfully invaded Italy, Constantine launched a battle against Emperor Maxentius on 28 October AD 312. Prior to this battle, tradition tells us, Constantine saw a cross in the sky with the words "*In Hoc Signo Vinces*" ("with this sign shall you conquer"). While Christians contend that it was a crucifix in the sky, many scholars disagree claiming that it was actually the Chi-Ro symbol latterly used as a seal of the emperor. Whether a cross or letters, the fact remains that this vision, one of many experienced by the emperor in his lifetime, has supported a legend that Constantine converted to Christianity on the spot. Whether this story had any validity is not known though it is a fact that as early as the year AD 313 Constantine was making public proclamations that showed a distinct change in official Roman policy in favour of Christianity. In particular, Constantine's Edict of Milan, which was made in agreement with Licinius, Emperor of the East, set out provisions of absolute tolerance of Christianity. This edict demanded the return of confiscated property to the Christians and ended over a decade of persecution started in AD 306 by Diocletian.

By 325 Constantine was an open supporter of the faith and was endeavouring to bring together the strings of the various sects of Christianity to form one cohesive religion that could be turned to the advantage of the State. It was at this time that he convened the Council of Nicea which eventually declared the aims, objectives and, of course, the rules of what was to become the accepted religion of the whole Roman world. Those who could not agree with the final directions springing from Nicea were at first marginalized and eventually persecuted. It soon became Constantine's profound belief that there should be only one recognized Church within the Roman State.

Undoubtedly, Constantine realized that to capture the heart of a group of peoples as disparate as those who lived under Roman rule was a difficult matter, though to "own" their souls would make life very much easier. A state-run religion, especially when its priesthood was directly responsible to the emperor himself, would assure Constantine and future emperors of a better ordered and less fractionalized society within which the State could operate. Christianity, still in a fairly "plastic" state, offered the best chance of achieving these ideals and those who opposed this line of thinking were ruthlessly sought out and destroyed.

Paradoxically for a faith that was to centre on Rome for much of the next 1,500 years, Constantine turned his back on the city, choosing instead for his capital Constantinople, the city of Byzantium that had been renamed in his honour. However this move was for generally political reasons and there is no doubt that Rome remained the spiritual and emotional hub of the Empire. Since it was also recognized as the place of retreat of St Peter and the ultimate destination of St Paul, Rome was a natural focal point for Christianity. In any case for many centuries the Holy Land itself lay beyond the sway of Christian rulers.

We are often led to believe, particularly by religiously motivated historians, that what emerged after Constantine was Roman Catholic Christianity, but nothing could be further from the truth. It was some three or four centuries after Constantine that anything even approaching Roman Catholicism emerged. The legacy that Constantine left was a pattern of Churches, each calling itself Christian and each sharing a basic set of values and beliefs. But when it came to actual worship it was accepted that each Christian community would interpret the Gospels in its own way and behave as local custom and consideration of Christianity dictated.

Through the remainder of Roman rule in France and Britain, Christianity prospered to a greater or lesser degree. In the case of England there are many examples of local place names that retain elements suggesting that Christian shrines and churches of ultimately Roman foundation once existed. This is especially true in the case of "Eccles" type names which are widespread especially in parts of northeastern England. Exactly what took place in these locations we have no way of knowing, but local churches, probably of wood, seem to have been built and some very early monastic-type institutions may also have existed. There is a persistent insistence in local folklore that York, on account of its associations with Constantine (and especially his mother Helena), was the first truly important Christian city in Britain.

Of particular interest with this regard are a whole series of churches which stand to the west of York, occupying the rough boundaries of a small Celtic kingdom known as Elmet. This had been one of the "*civitatis*" or regions of the larger tribal kingdom of Brigantia at the time of the Roman arrival in Britain. Even after Roman rule it maintained its integrity well into the advent of Anglo-Saxon domination.

Still to be found spread around the boundaries of old Elmet are a number of ancient churches with the dedication of "All Saints". Local tradition has it that all these churches were set up by St Helena herself. These persistent historical rumours might be worth little were it not for the fact that there is also a proliferation of sacred well sites in the same geographical region which is known to this day as St Helen's Wells.

One of the All Saints churches, at Otley, not far from Leeds and twenty or so miles from York, was much altered in Victorian times. During the restoration work the floor of the church was lifted and it became possible to trace the foundations of a much earlier church beneath the present edifice. The dimensions of this chapel were identical with other Romano-Celtic churches of a very early date identified in other parts of England.

During the excavation of a path along the side of the churchyard in Otley, Christian-type burials were disturbed, some of which contained coins of the period of Diocletian. It will be recalled that the life of Constantine was contemporary with Diocletian, whose coins would still have been in circulation during Constantine's own reign. This may serve to add at least circumstantial evidence to the theory that the Elmet churches were founded by Constantine's family and in particular his mother Helena.

Be that as it may, there is also some reason to believe that Christianity was flourishing in parts of Britain even well before Constantine's reign. Tradition has it that a group of people fleeing the Holy Land at the time of the Jewish uprising came to what is now Glastonbury in Somerset and were granted land.

It is suggested that the king of the area gave these very early Christians (if this is what they actually were) ten hides of land. Again this may be nonsense, but the *Doomsday Book* of 1086 clearly states that the church in Glastonbury controlled ten hides of land upon which tax had never been paid, so there is some reason to believe that the story may be based on a genuine and very early event.

It would have been quite natural for Jews escaping the worst excesses of Roman retribution to flee to places as far from the centre of the Empire as Britain. In this remote place they could have remained more or less undetected by the local authorities who may, in any case, have been quite happy to leave them alone if they were not representing a threat to local peace or prosperity. Scotland and Ireland remained absolutely beyond the sway of Rome throughout the entire period so these areas, though generally wild and governed by tribal lords, may also have represented a place of relatively safe, if somewhat uncomfortable, exile.

The same sort of situation was generally true in Gaul. The area was large and much of it remote marshy or mountainous terrain. It would have been impossible for the Roman authorities to know the exact ethnic origin of such widely spread populations. The southern cities of Gaul, such as Marseilles, were already famous trading ports which would have been as familiar with Jews as they were with peoples from all over the Empire. It is quite likely that hundreds, if not thousands, of those escaping the Roman onslaught on Judea, and later peoples suffering under anti-Christian persecutions, would have found a safe home in either Gaul or Britain.

In both Britain and Gaul, Roman occupation had done very little to eradicate indigenous belief patterns. Roman rule was very tolerant of local beliefs, and deities dear to the heart of any specific people would generally find a counterpart amongst the rich Roman pantheon. All of Britain and large parts of Gaul was peopled by Celts during the Roman occupation. The original spiritual leaders of these people had been the Druids, a species of itinerant priests and lawgivers that the Romans generally distrusted.

The word Druid probably derives from a term that means "oak man" and it is true that oak groves were particularly sacred to Celtic peoples. The Celts were great nature worshippers and gave reverence to numerous types of trees, together with water sources such as wells and springs, rivers and lakes.

The Druids had a long and illustrious history. Members of this priestly class were often drawn from the selfsame families of chieftains who ruled the various Celtic tribes, much as younger sons of later aristocratic families were encouraged to join the Christian priesthood. Druid aspirants trained at "colleges" from a very early age, often for twenty years or so before being considered proficient in their occupation. They were at liberty to wander from place to place dispensing astronomical, religious and legal advice and negotiating treaties in times of war, which were numerous amongst the fractious Celtic tribes.

With the Roman occupation of Gaul and Britain, the authorities considered that the itinerant nature of the Druidic presence within the local society made them likely candidates for stirring up insurrection against the Roman overlords. For this reason, the Druids were persecuted at every opportunity. Even when Gaul had been successfully annexed, it was suggested that new Druids, trained in Britain, were constantly being shipped into the area. Indeed one of Julius Caesar's, and later Claudius's avowed reasons for invading Britain was to finally eradicate the danger posed to Roman rule by the Druidic colleges.

The forces of Claudius, invading Britain in AD 43, raced up through southern England and thence into Wales. Their target was the island known today as Anglesey. This was a place of immense importance to the Celts generally and to the Druids in particular. Their name for the island was Inis Mona (Sacred Island) and it was suggested that it was in Anglesey that the Druidic colleges were located. However, since Ireland remained indomitable to the Romans, and as their attempts to subjugate Scotland also came to nothing, it is unlikely that the

Romans ever managed to eradicate the Druids from Celtic life. It is possible that the early arrival of an early and "flexible" form of Christianity to the shores of Britain offered remaining Druids a more or less legitimate way to ply their chosen profession. There is little to differentiate the earliest Culdean Celtic preachers (eventually monks) from the itinerant Druids, and even the form of tonsure or haircut that the Druids are known to have sported was common to the early Culdeans.

Where this very early group of wandering Christian preachers originated is completely unknown. Because of the success of later Irish and Scottish Celtic missionaries in the conversion of Anglo-Saxon England, it is generally assumed that Ireland and Scotland were Christianized prior to England. This is patently not the case since Roman Christianity flourished for some centuries in England. It is more likely that Culdeans present in England after the withdrawal of the Roman legions in the sixth century may have been driven out. Alternatively they were forced underground by the pagan hoards of the Anglo-Saxons pouring into the country at the time. The time after the Roman withdrawal from Britain is aptly named the Dark Ages and we have very little reliable historical evidence of events that took place for at least a couple of centuries. It is during this period that we first encounter St Patrick, an interesting character for several reasons. Certainly today he is the patron saint of Ireland and the Christianization of the Anglo-Saxons is generally credited to Celtic monks following in his wake (people such as Columba). However, even the legends assert that St Patrick was of English, and not Irish, blood and that he was instrumental in bringing Christianity to Ireland from the mainland.

Patrick is said to have been born to a Romano-British family at a village called Bannavem, the location of which is not now known. His father was called Calpurnius and Patrick found his way to Ireland after being captured by a band of pirates raiding the west coast of England. The supposed year of Patrick's birth is around 389, which places him well within the Romano-

British period and not so long after the reign of Constantine.

Sold into slavery in Ireland, and for six years working as a shepherd, Patrick finally escaped, possibly to Gaul. Returning to Britain for a spell, he then seems to have become a monk at the monastery of Lerins in what is today France. After this, he returned to Ireland to succeed a previous Christian missionary by the name of Paulinus. There he eventually succeeded in Christianizing most of the island and started a cult that has flourished ever since. St Patrick died in the year 461.

Some sixty years later a native Irishman, Columba, was destined to become one of the most influential characters in western European Christianity. High-born of the Irish royal family, Columba was eventually forced, by the warring tribes of which he was a part, to flee to Scotland. There, on the remote island of Iona, he founded what was destined to become one of the most important monasteries in the world.

From Columbia's incursion into Scotland sprang the monastic ideals that were to spread Christianity right through the northern Anglo-Saxons who after his time were consolidating their hold on England. However, any comparison between the form of Christianity practised by Columba and his contemporaries and that which followed later in western Europe may well be erroneous. St Columba, for all his supposed piety, was a Culdean Christian of Celtic stock. His natural home, in true Celtic tradition, was close to water, under the great vault of heaven and surrounded by nature. Although he preached the Christian Gospels, like his fellow Culdeans he sought remote and wild places in which to live and venerated nature in all its forms. They were wild men, born of wild places and times, and they undoubtedly had much in common with the Druids who had been their forefathers.

Even the word "Culdean" has an interesting etymology for it is said to mean "the strangers amongst us". There are many explanations as to how this expression came about, but it is generally held that it is of a date much earlier than that of Columba himself, and it may be responsive to the arrival of groups such as those of the Essene shortly after the Jewish uprising of AD 70. In the case of the first early Christians to arrive in Glastonbury, England, it is said that they mixed freely with, and learned much from, the Druidic community of the area where they settled. Whether fact or fiction, this story serves to illustrate that there were known connections between Druidism and Culdean Christianity from the very start. Like the Druids, the Culdeans were the repository of tribal wisdom. It is highly likely that even the Druids had inherited their learning and power from even earlier "priests" already incumbent in Britain at the time the Celts arrive in these islands during the Iron Age. As a result, we may see in the Culdeans the legatees of many thousands of years of religion and learning in the far west of Europe.

Later Latin monks complained bitterly about the practices and true beliefs of the Culdean Christians and accused them of every imaginable form of heresy. These disputes between the established Church and the slightly renegade version in the islands of Britain came to a head on many occasions, but most notably during the Synod of Whitby in the year 655.

The circumstances that led to the Synod of Whitby are important in the context of our story, though the result has often been vastly overplayed. Following the death of Columba, the Culdean Church continued to flourish in Iona in Scotland. From here, at the invitation of Oswald, the Anglo-Saxon king of Northumbria, a monk named Aiden was dispatched to bring Christianity to Oswald's people. He established himself on the remote and beautiful island of Lindisfarne on the northeast coast of England in the year 635, some forty years after the death of Columba. All went well until a few decades later, during the reign of King Oswiu, when a dispute broke out regarding matters relating to the celebration of certain Christian festivals. King Oswiu's wife, Elflaeda, was from the south of England and was a legatee of Christian missionaries from the Continent. Many of the dates of the "Latin Christian" celebrations were different than those of the Irish and Scottish Church and this caused some consternation within the royal household because Oswiu was a Christian of Culdean descent.

To try and sort matters out once and for all, a meeting or Synod was held in Whitby in 663 and 664. The result is reported as having been a triumph for the Latin Christians, for King Oswiu ruled that their practices should henceforth prevail in his realm. Almost any orthodox historical handling of these events will leave the reader with the impression that here was a defeat of a kind of pagan-affected Culdean Christianity by the forces of the Roman Church. This is a completely erroneous view and a misunderstanding of Church history in the far west of Europe. Although some of the Culdean representatives of the Whitby Synod went home to Scotland in something of a sulk they had lost virtually nothing, except their own calculation for the date of Easter together with a change of hairstyle to that more regularly worn on the Continent. The modern Roman Catholic Church may claim that the Synod of Whitby was a turning point in British Christianity, but this is not the case. What those making this assertion fail to understand is that the Roman Catholic Church they represent did not exist in Britain, or in fact anywhere else, for some two centuries after the Synod of Whitby.

At this date in Christianity, no church was absolutely bound by the sort of rigid rules that eventually came to be the case with Catholicism. The Celts were still fully at liberty to worship as they pleased as long as they could show that they conformed to the general principles and doctrines of the Mother Church as a whole. Celtic church services were not celebrated in Latin and probably did not take the same form as those practised in Rome. The monastic ideal of Culdean Christianity was vastly different from that of the Latin monks of the same period. Culdeans sought solitude and contemplation in remote places, keeping to a monastic ideal almost identical with the earlier Essene and the later Cistercians. They wandered around, as the Druids had done, preaching at wayside crosses or in tiny chapels known as "*loca sancta*". The idea of large cathedrals or vast stone monasteries would have been totally alien to them and only much later did this state of affairs change.

Many Culdean foundations were placed upon the same longitudinal and latitudinal Salt Lines that had been revered in Britain since time out of hand (see chapter 1). Lindisfarne is one example out of many, as is the enchanting church at Lastingham in North Yorkshire.

Representatives of the Culdean saints were often drawn from ancient Salt Line families that were almost certainly of pre-Celtic stock. Where it had been necessary to convert an indigenous population to Christianity, local pagan Celtic deities were invariably incorporated into church practices and rituals. There are many Celtic saints whose ancestry is distinctly pagan. A good example would be that of Brigit who is clearly a Christianized version of Brigantia, the tutelary deity of the largest Celtic tribe in Britain, who in deference to their patron goddess were known by the Romans as the Brigantes. This is merely one example out of hundreds and there are still many instances where one or two local churches in parts of Britain and Ireland still carry the dedication of a saint whose biography is completely unknown in terms of Christian history. The life history of such "saints" has been fabricated to lay a veneer of acceptability over their pagan past.

At about the same time as the Synod of Whitby the Christianization of France was taking place. As was the case in Britain, Christianity had made some inroads into Gaul during the Roman period but the full sway of the religion did not take place until the early sixth century, under the auspices of the Frankish Merovingian King Clovis. Unlike England, which lost much of its Roman Christianity during the early Anglo-Saxon period, France never reverted after the time of Clovis, though the form of Christianity did change at a later date. Clovis opted for a form of Christianity not entirely unlike that practised today but this brought him into conflict with peoples living in the area today known as Burgundy. Many of the Burgundians were Arians, a version of Christianity that, for some time, gained much ground. Arianism existed even before Constantine's Council of Nicea, but the name under which we know it today is a direct response to the name of the man who would be held a heretic for his view of Christianity.

Arius was the presbyter of Alexandria and began to spread his views between AD 319 and 322. He held to the belief that Jesus was not of the "same substance" as God and therefore could not "be" God. The dispute was a major part of the Council of Nicea and was a debate between Arius and his rival Athanasius. The Athanasius camp held that Jesus was *Ahomoousios*, or the same substance as God, while the Arians under Arius contended that Jesus was *Ahomoiousios*, or like God but not of the same substance as God. The difference in the two Greek words was far more significant than the single letter *iota* that separates them. The debate ran on and on for days with the Athanasius camp ruling the day and thus the opinion and dogma of the Church. This victory would see the positioning of Jesus into the Trinity and it is the Nicean Creed that came out of the council that is still recited by Roman Catholics worldwide.

Arianism failed to gain any ground during or after the life of King Clovis and so ceased to exist as a viable alternative to what we would now term as Catholic Christianity. However, it would be fair to say that during the reign of Clovis and his direct descendants the Christianity practised throughout much of France was similar to that of Britain. Culdeans, such as Columba, had achieved a degree of influence on the Continent and even very early English saints from the Roman period, such as St Alban, are known to have been venerated at the court of Clovis.

All was well in Frankish Gaul until the reign of Dagobert II. He was the last of the truly Merovingian monarchs and held the throne between AD 673 and 676. The kingship of Dagobert did not last long and yet it represents one of the most important departures in the story of the Cistercian and the Knights Templar. As a result of Dagobert's death, a cauldron of conflicting ideas and interests came about. Amidst the ensuing turmoil, the old Salt Line families of France and Britain embarked on an initiative that nearly turned Europe completely on its head. The ultimate result of their efforts was the creation of the Cistercians and their armed brothers, the Templars.

Chapter 6

The Pattern Emerges

A direct descendant of Clovis, the first Christian king of the Franks, Dagobert was "born in interesting times", as says the Chinese curse. Dagobert was the son of Sigebert III and was born in about 650. His father having died at a relatively young age, and the Frankish kingdom being in a state of some ferment, the young Dagobert was packed off to a monastery in Ireland in 656. The reason for this state of affairs was factional fighting within and around the Frankish royal family. The Merovingian kings, from before the time of Clovis, had ruled with the aid of certain court officials often known as Mayors of the Palace. These agencies became more and more powerful and were prone to seeking the throne for themselves. This was precisely the state of affairs that endured during Dagobert's infancy and he was probably lucky to escape with his life. During this period the kingdom of Clovis was split into Austrasia and Neustrasia. Austrasia was Dagobert's birthright but Childebert the Adopted, son of Grimoald, the Mayor of the Palace, usurped his throne. Dagobert's cousin, Clotaire III eventually overthrew Childebert and gave the throne of Austrasia to Childeric II in the year 662. Childeric was assassinated in 665 and a search was made for Dagobert, who was at last recognized as the rightful king of Austrasia.

By this time, Dagobert was most certainly in England where he had gained some recognition amongst the Culdean monks who inhabited the relatively new monastery of Lindisfarne. It was with the help of the Culdeans that Dagobert was located and shipped home to Austrasia. The young king returned to France espousing a form of Christianity that for some reason infuriated the ruling powers of the Vatican. This might have been partly due to the fact that he almost immediately married Giselle, the daughter of a Visigoth king from southern France. The Visigoths at the time were either not Christian at all or else Arian heretics. In truth, the reasons for the Vatican's dislike of Dagobert are not fully understood, but of the enmity that existed between them there is little room for doubt.

The Church of Rome had declared a perpetual alliance with Clovis at the time he had adopted Christianity as the state religion of his extensive Frankish kingdoms. This mutual "bargain" had been intended to extend to the heirs of Clovis, but it seems to have been simply forgotten in the case of Dagobert II.

It is now largely accepted that the assassination of Dagobert in the forest of Stenay in 679 is attributable to the Vatican, or at least was carried out with its sanction. We have seen that there was a suggestion prevalent that the family of Giselle, Dagobert's Visigoth wife, were Arians, a faction that was taken very seriously by the established Church. It is possible that the authorities in Rome considered that Dagobert might, following the marriage, begin to demonstrate Arian tendencies.

A far more likely scenario is that, having spent so much time in Ireland and England, Dagobert had been deeply affected by the Culdean Church. Elements of this church were still smarting from the decisions made at the Whitby Synod of 664, just a few months before Dagobert returned to Austrasia. The same Culdean Christians, whose values were being eroded by Rome at the Synod of Whitby, were also represented in Ireland where Dagobert had also spent some time. The Frankish kingdoms of Old Gaul were the foremost bastions of orthodox Roman

Christianity at the time and the Vatican may have panicked if it had reason to believe that a Celtic-indoctrinated, Culdean Christian king had taken root in Austrasia.

Rome was accused, at the time and since, of having at least sanctioned the murder of Dagobert II. Whether this is an unfair accusation or not, the Vatican certainly wholeheartedly endorsed the cause of the Carolingian king who took the place of the Merovingian Dagobert. And it was with the accession of the later Carolingian monarch Charlemagne in 768 that true Roman Catholicism and feudalism were born: this in turn sowed the seeds of the ultimate demise of Culdean-type Christianity.

We are cognizant that at this point in our story at least some readers will be noting that we are dealing with matters that are similar to those discussed by the writers Baigent, Leigh and Lincoln in their famous book *The Holy Blood and the Holy Grail*. One of the main objectives of that book was to explore the possibility of the existence, from the time of the death of Dagobert II onwards, of a mysterious fraternity whose express desire was to return the rightful Merovingian dynasty to the throne of France. The body in question is known as the Prieure de Sion and it was, suggested Baigent, Leigh and Lincoln, instrumental in numerous events in European history since the eighth century, which were geared towards achieving this ultimate objective.

We shall have more to say about the Prieure de Sion in due course but for the moment it is worth relating that the mouth-pieces of the supposed modern Prieure de Sion declared to the writers of *The Holy Blood and the Holy Grail* that they consider the Merovingian kings to have been of the direct bloodline of Jesus himself. This admittedly far-fetched assertion is inextricably tied to a popular myth that Mary Magdalene, supposedly the wife of Jesus, arrived in France shortly after the crucifixion, bearing the son of Jesus. He, it is said, married into the early Merovingian families of France, thus preserving the "line of David" through to Clovis I and his heirs.

Whilst we find it impossible to test these assertions in the absence of any hard evidence, the supposed continuum of Merovingian support identified by Baigent, Leigh and Lincoln does bear out certain sections of our own evidence base. However, it is only fair to indicate that the "bloodline of Christ", as suggested in *The Holy Blood and the Holy Grail*, is not the only possible explanation for the continued existence of a group or faction that might have appeared to be dedicated to the restoration of the Merovingian dynasty. Whether or not some, or part, of this faction has (at some historical period) chosen to call itself the Prieure de Sion is a moot point. However we often found ourselves following a historical track that at least ran parallel with that followed by Baigent, Leigh and Lincoln and we would by no means rule out the existence of such a body, either in the past or in more recent times.

With the advent of the Carolingian kings, and particularly with the crowning of Charlemagne in 768, western European Christianity underwent a sea change that was to prove more than a simple religious diversion. The Carolingians were often at odds with both the old guard of Roman Christianity and the form of government that the Roman Empire had originally inspired. On very many occasions, the Carolingians directly attacked Latin thinking. The old divisions of government (*civitatis*) originally established by Rome were abolished and were replaced by an emerging "feudal" system. Many of the Latin Christians were persecuted, some of them being shipped out of the old *civitatis* to become mere "villains" or serfs within the feudal economy.

Broadly speaking, feudalism, as it evolved amongst the Carolingian Franks, was a response to the collapse of Roman-style rule. With no legions to protect the state as a whole, it was left to the nominal rulers of such areas to devise their own strategy. Feudalism was one of the most frequent responses. In this system rulers, invariably but not always kings, would pass gifts of land to powerful agencies in return for their support in times of war. The feudal state, in simple terms, was like a huge pyramid with the king sitting at its apex. The great lords below the king owed him allegiance which was meted out in terms of taxes and military support. These same lords ruled the lower aristocracy who formed the backbone of the whole system. They in turn controlled manors that were peopled by several classes of commoners. From lowest to highest in the feudal pecking order every individual owed something to the next highest link in the chain. The lowest class (the villains) farmed land that was held by their lord and paid him rent on this land in cash or kind. Alongside the serfs, freemen held land that belonged to them, but still found themselves responsible to a manorial lord, to whom a quarterly or annual debt was payable.

Some of the moneys received by the manorial lords was passed back up the pyramid and eventually reached the monarch who controlled an exchequer and to whom, ultimately, a duty to fight in times of war was also written into the bargain.

Invariably, the nature of the feudal system led to disagreements and warfare at all levels as the barons fought with each other over perceived family rights or simply because they were strong enough to do so. In the end it was the common herd that suffered and which formed the backbone of a ramshackle infantry in times of war.

Feudalism inspired greed at all levels and it wasn't long before even land owned by the Church was being parcelled out by the Frankish kings. This displeased the Church, as did the perpetual argument over who should appoint priests in given areas: the local ecclesiastical authorities or the local lord. In England at least, this latter dilemma was a persistent sore and only finally ceased to be a problem between monarch and Church after the Reformation. In the fullness of time, the Frankish feudalism inspired a more severe form of repression upon the lower classes than they had previously known, and this started to be reflected in the form of developing Christianity. "Uniformity" became the key word, with an eventual insistence that Church masses were of a particular sort and that they were celebrated in Latin. The vernacular was eventually eradicated entirely from the business of the Church. Church dogma became more and more entrenched and eventually was not merely forced upon worshippers at a not just local but even international level.

At first, and perhaps in a way that now seems paradoxical, Rome kicked against such changes, but the power of the Franks ultimately prevailed and Roman Catholicism was the result. The Franks conquered territory far beyond the original borders of their homeland, extending down into northern Italy and threatening the autonomy of the Vatican. Ultimately feudal values were passed to the emerging Normans who in turn carried the principles, together with the now fully developed Roman Catholicism, to England after the Conquest of 1066.

Faced with a *fait accompli* forced upon them by the tremendously powerful Franks, even local rulers who may have naturally disagreed with the principles of feudal government had little option but to fall in line. It is our considered opinion that there were many such individuals. In addition it is obvious that there were numerous agencies within the Church, especially that of Anglo-Saxon England and the Celtic margins of Scotland, Wales and Ireland, that would have shuddered at the restrictions imposed by Roman Catholicism (more properly Frankish Catholicism).

In order to see why this might be the case, we need to look more closely at the sort of government and Church authorities that had prevailed previously, not only in Britain but also within the Frankish homelands and their surroundings.

In terms of the Church itself, it has often been cited (mostly by Roman Catholic historians themselves) that one of the reasons for the survival of the Catholic Church relies on the fact that it has learned to adapt itself to the circumstances of the people with whom it comes into contact. This may be true up to a point, but in terms of the west of Europe any such accommodation had already taken place well ahead of the Carolingians. The Celts in particular were a proud people with a rich religious heritage of their own. Celts have never taken kindly to subjugation, no matter from what direction it has come. Opposition to Roman rule never ceased in some parts of the Celtic British Isles, but at least the Romans had done little (except in the suppression of the Druids) to try and indoctrinate the Celts into alternative religious practices.

The same was probably also true of sections of the populations that fell under the heel of the Frankish monarchs. This was particularly so with regard to the people of Burgundy whose origins were far from the centre of France. The Burgundians do not seem to have settled willingly either for the feudal system or for an imposed form of restrictive and sterile religion.

From the perspective of the average peasant living almost anywhere in the far west of Europe at the time, it is difficult to see how they would have registered the change from Roman patterns of government to feudal ones to any great degree. It was in the lower ranks of the ruling classes that the changes would be felt to the greatest degree and in particular to those who took it upon themselves to be the religious, legal and historical mouthpieces of their respective cultures.

Slowly, but certainly, it appears that a deep resentment concerning the imposed changes was beginning to ferment both within the borders of the Frankish lands and, later, within Britain. Such was the nature of feudalism, and so powerful the voice of the Roman Catholic Church, that there appeared to be little that could be done to redress the balance. However, it is our profound belief that steps were being taken amongst a cohesive and ancient group of ruling families in and around France, and within Britain, to find ways to counter the rising tide of feudal rule. Agencies existed that would attempt to counter the evermore severe impositions of faith and practice from an alien and remote Church hierarchy.

The proof of these extraordinary assertions is to be found amongst those peoples who had inhabited the old megalithic Salt Line locations since time out of mind. Ultimately, the response to both feudalism and to the more restrictive Church practices was to be exemplified by a number of Salt Line confederations from across the whole of France, Flanders and Britain. However, the initial impetus came from one particular region and from a fairly closed circle of individuals within a few regionally powerful families. Alan had previously noticed how many modern French cities occupied Salt Line positions. These include Reims, Lille, Rouen, Caen, Sens, Nantes, Besançon and a host of other examples. And though all these locations will become important to our story in the fullness of time, it is to the cities of Dijon, capital of Burgundy, and especially to Troyes, capital of Champagne, that we must first turn our attention.

It was from these cities and their surrounding regions that we first recognized the historical impetus growing that would eventually emerge as an attempt to hijack western European Christianity. It would, in time, lead to the evolution of the Europe we know today. It is our intention to tell this story as fully as evidence allows, but first it would be sensible to explain what might have been "special" or "different" regarding the aristocratic families of these two regions. The explanation has much to do with the historical origins of these people.

For the realization of the following information, we are deeply indebted to Henry Lincoln, co-writer of *The Holy Blood and the Holy Grail* and also the author of numerous other books which represent an alternative view of much of European history. His assistance to our cause was offered one weekend at a lively seminar at Gullane in Edinburgh, Scotland. When writers come together, sparks often fly and it is truly amazing how frequently the most casual comment can start one thinking down an alternative road that leads to some surprising destinations.

We had been giving a lecture on some of our initial ideas regarding the Knights Templar and their origins, and had made specific reference to the regions of Burgundy and Champagne. Henry Lincoln listened attentively but it wasn't until the next day that he approached us. By that time, we had heard his own lecture which detailed some of his astounding discoveries together with those of the Danish researcher and television director, Erling Haagensen. Henry Lincoln has been fascinated for decades with certain geometric patterns associated in partic- ular with the region around the mysterious little southern French village of Rennes le Château. After the publication of some of his findings, Erling Haagensen had contacted Henry concerning a number of similar discoveries of his own, but ones that were made far from the arid landscape of the Razes.

Haagensen has a particular interest in the island of Bornholm which is located in the Baltic Sea and is now Danish territory. He had discovered certain geometric patterns on Bornholm that appeared to be related to a series of fifteen churches, all of which were built in the thirteenth century and some of which appeared to be Templar (or Templar-type) foundations. The arrangement of the churches implied an attempt on the part of the builders to etch a neat series of pentagonal designs across and around the island.

Henry Lincoln told Erling Haagensen that he considered the patterns he had found around Rennes le Château to be signifi- cantly older than the thirteenth century and asked if Bornholm contained any structures or relics from the megalithic period. Haagensen confirmed that the island was replete with them and that many were associated with the church buildings, even being incorporated into the fabric of the thirteenth-century structures.

Lincoln explained that during his subsequent research into Bornholm he had discovered a little known fact. Although Bornholm is only a very small island, about 588 sq. km, it managed to create one of the most powerful kingdoms of post- Roman Europe. The original name for Bornholm was Burgundarsholm and it was people from the island that had been responsible for the creation of Burgundy.

In the first century of the modern era, these people had moved first to the lower valley of the Vistula River. They came to be skilled auxiliaries in the Roman army, and by the fifth century AD they had already established what came to be a powerful kingdom. In the west, it extended to the River Rhine but was centred upon what is now Savoy and took in Lake Geneva.

With the Roman decline in western Europe, the Burgundian control increased until it encompassed most of Savoy and ultimately the Saone and Rhone River valleys. Even after the Franks overthrew the independent Burgundy, it still covered a huge area. The carve-up of land after the death of Clotaire I, circa 561, found Burgundy classified as "Regnum Burgundiae". It was a vast area and included much territory in north-central France, including much of what came to be known eventually as Champagne and particularly the great city of Troyes.

Henry Lincoln had recognized from our work a historically supported assertion on our part that even as late as the twelfth century there were ruling agencies in the areas of modern France that maintained a direct and unbroken link with the megalithic cultures. These had flourished in a wide arc across Scandinavia, Britain and parts of France, together with eastern and southern Spain, extending well down into the islands of the Mediterranean.

As far as the Burgundians and the people of Champagne were concerned, the megalithic roots were easy to ascertain and had been pure Scandinavian in origin. We now knew for certain that the ancestors of these people had come from a location where megalithic endeavour had been evident and where a much later, but equally fascinating, Templar presence had been established.

The first sign that something "special" was beginning to develop in these regions comes with the tremendous push that was evident in the area for the organization of a crusade on the Holy Land.

The Reasons for the First Crusade
To itemize a single reason for the launching of the First Crusade, which came about as a direct result of a call to arms by Pope Urban II in 1095, is impossible. To a great extent it was a product of a mixture of the rising success of some Western

powers, the increasing incursions of Muslims into Christian territory and the rising popularity of pilgrimage. The circumstances that made the crusade a viable proposition might be somewhat easier to identify however.

Towards the end of the eleventh century, the population of western Europe was growing rapidly. The rise in feudalism had led to the creation of numerous major and minor aristocratic families, many of which had large numbers of sons, only a few of whom could hope to inherit the family estates. Surplus sons, often brought up in a heady religious environment and with tales of an impending apocalypse ringing in their ears, were looking for some glorious quest in which to take part. Tales of chivalry, no matter how misplaced they were in the generally cruel and even vicious ruling classes of western Europe, were popular and the age of the armed knight was at its zenith.

Meanwhile in the Middle East, the Seljuk Turks were causing great problems to eastern Christians and there were repeated requests made of successive popes for aid to be dispatched to beleaguered forces in this area and that.

In addition to these and a whole selection of other factors, the Vatican may have had its own particular interest in "inventing" a reason to empty the West, temporarily, of a large proportion of its fighting men. The very nature of feudalism continually led to open warfare on both a large and a smaller scale. This invariably proved difficult in one way or another for the Church. The pope probably reasoned that a large-scale war in the Middle East would allay some of the difficulties encountered in France particularly, and that it might "thin out" a little the number of potential "armed thugs" who had little else to do but fight with one another.

The main reason identified at the time for launching a crusade against the Turks was the simple expedient of freeing the Holy Land for the passage of pilgrims to and from Jerusalem and the other holy sites. These days we are inclined to be cynical regarding the actions of almost any power-broking authority, but perhaps in this case such cynicism would be unjust. Certainly the Muslim authorities at the time did not prevent Christian pilgrims from entering the Holy City, but it was suggested that their passage between the seaports of the Levant and Jerusalem itself was becoming more and more dangerous.

Although it was the pope himself (Urban II) who finally called for a crusade to be launched at Clermont-Ferrand in 1095, there is no way of knowing precisely what pressures he may have been under from his advisors or the monarchs of Christian countries that fell within the scope of his influence. What might be quite telling, in view of the information that follows, is that Odo of Chatillon-sur-Marne, which was Urban II's real name, was a Frenchman and a native of Champagne. He was of noble stock and so would therefore have family ties with a sizeable group of other individuals about whom we shall learn more in due course. What may or may not also be significant is the knowledge that Clermont-Ferrand, the city in south-central France outside the city walls of which he called for the crusade, is bisected by a longitudinal Salt Line. However, we may not necessarily take this last fact as being evidence of anything except that, against all the odds of probability, so many French towns and cities are on Salt Lines.

What intrigued us so much with regard to the actual organization and prosecution of the First Crusade was how much support was offered by a specific group of individuals who could be shown to be ultimately of Burgundian and Champagne origin. This fact they shared with Urban II himself, but the ancestry of the people in question showed them to have been born of Salt Line families of great antiquity.

Foremost amongst these people has to be Godfroi de Bouillon, Count of Lorraine. Godfroi was descended from the Emperor Charlemagne, but he also had much older, Merovingian blood in his veins. He came from Bouillon in the Ardennes, now in Belgium, which is a longitudinal Salt Line city and he was closely related to the rulers of Burgundy. Godfroi was deeply religious. He grew to be tall, fair-haired and was thought to be the perfect Christian knight. He is said to have given up all his lands and to have sacrificed his titles to embark on the First Crusade, and it was Godfroi who led the successful final assault on Jerusalem on 15 July 1099.

Of Godfroi's success as an administrator little can be said that would be favourable, but he knew how to fight and to lead men into battle. Undoubtedly his role in the capture of Jerusalem had been very important, so much so that he was offered the crown of Jerusalem within days of its capture. He refused the title of king, but maintained the rights and privileges on offer. Unfortunately, he did not enjoy them for long as he was soon dead, probably as a result of poison. The crown of Jerusalem was then offered to his brother Baudoin, also from Bouillon, who became Baudoin I of Jerusalem.

While these monumental events were taking place in the far off Levant, a previously shadowy group of individuals, centred on Troyes, part of old Burgundy but by this time capital of the Duchy of Champagne, were laying down their own plans. Troyes was an ancient Salt Line city of some distinction by the end of the eleventh century and was run as a virtually independent state, though one allied to the French crown. The Count of Champagne was Hugh, a man of learning and culture. He lived in a great palace in the middle of his city of merchants and churches, where embryonic schools and university-type institutions were already spreading the values of education and chivalry.

Hugh de Champagne was so typical of the sort of French noble that gladly took part in the First Crusade that it might seem surprising that he was not included in Godfroi's vanguard. It seems that he had other plans at the time, and ones that would fulfil the destiny he held in common with a number of other individuals that were his family and friends. (Actually, as we shall see, it is entirely possible that Hugh de Champagne was in Jerusalem in 1099) One of these was a kinsman by the name of Hugh de Payens. He held a fiefdom in northwest Troyes from the count and lived in the city. His name is unknown to history before the end of the eleventh century and so we have very little information to offer regarding his lineage except his blood relationship with the Count of Champagne.

A third member of this group was André de Montbard. He was also related to Count Hugh and, perhaps more importantly, he was the uncle of the Cistercian abbot later to be canonized St Bernard. Bernard of Clairvaux would play an important role in Salt Line affairs and in particular the order of the Temple as we shall examine in due course. André de Montbard came from a rich and powerful family who took their name from a town in Burgundy, not too far from Dijon, though the family had extensive holdings in both Burgundy and Champagne. Like all noblemen of the period no doubt, André perambulated about between his estates, though his preferred residence also seemed to have been in Troyes.

These men, together with others, some named and some anonymous, were busy hatching their own plans as Godfroi de Bouillon, to whom they were also blood-tied, carved out a name for himself atop the broken walls of Jerusalem. This little conclave of Salt Line nobles had an idea, the germ of which was probably nurtured in other equally elevated but unknown breasts. We can imagine them meeting in the bright palace of Troyes (now long since demolished) and anxiously discussing the events that were unfolding so far away. To them, the happenings in the Middle East were a culmination of many generations of careful preparation and manipulation of political events. Like a great, virtually perpetual game of chess, piece by careful piece their game had been laid out. They were patient men, born of patient families, but they knew that they had a special destiny.

Deep in their hearts they bore a burning resentment for the Carolingian Franks and even for the Roman Catholic Church, though they willingly used both when it served their purposes to do so. No individual was too great or too small to be used as a pawn in this most important game, but they had to move with infinite care, as their fathers and their fathers' fathers had done, waiting until the time and circumstances were just right for their ultimate strategy to be put into play. The three men, Hugh de Champagne, Hugh de Payens and André de Montbard, together with a number of others whose faces will forever remain in the historical shadows, were planning to destroy once and for all the power of the established Church and to replace it with something far older and, to their way of thinking, more elevated. Through the decisions they made and the ultimate actions they took, they were destined to change the world forever, leaving the greatest Carolingian monarchs as mere footnotes of history. The story of their objectives and the methods they used to achieve them has never been fully explored until now.

Chapter 7

Towards a New Deal

Although Hugh, Count of Champagne and his colleagues in Troyes were destined to represent one of the most interesting strands of Burgundian Salt Line thinking in the years after the success of the First Crusade, they were merely following a prescribed path. It is very likely that the same family alliances had been involved in persuading Pope Urban II to call for the crusade in the first place for, as we have seen, Urban was from the area himself and must have received at least some support from the Champagne nobles. In addition, the group was clearly operating on other fronts to ensure that its overall objectives would eventually be met.

Whether or not this group of people was directly responsible for the formation of the Cistercian order, an event that is absolutely pivotal to our whole story, we cannot be certain. It could be that the embryonic monastic institution was merely "adopted" by the old Burgundian Salt Line families, but if this is the case there are a number of striking coincidences that remain unexplained.

Cistercianism, as it came to be known, was an ideal and one that found a fertile soil in Burgundy. Monasticism was nothing new to France or indeed to the Christian world as a whole in the eleventh century. On the contrary, the monastic ideal was thriving as it had, on and off, since the third century. Many, but by no means all, of the monks to be found in France during this period aspired to the Benedictine rule. This had been first laid down by St Benedict of Nursia, a fifth-century Italian who had himself embraced a monastic life and then assisted others to do so. St Benedict penned his "little rule for beginners" which itemized the ideal life for a would-be Christian monk and the circumstances under which he should live. The domestic arrangements suggested by St Benedict relied on old Roman and generally pre-Christian models of religious cohabitation. His instruction for the daily round of a monk encompassed periods of light work (in the house or abbey garden), balanced by long spells of communal religious services and personal meditation.

What St Benedict propounded was merely an ideal and even by the eleventh century, 400 years after his death, to be a Benedictine simply meant responding to a set of "standards". The Benedictine rule was certainly not written in stone and there was no cohesive authority until much later that could oversee the absolute adherence of its tenants. As a result, each abbey interpreted the rules in its own way and jealously guarded its own wealth and traditions. By the time of the First Crusade, many of the Benedictine abbeys had become lax in their adherence to the original conception that Benedict had laid down and this was a cause of great concern to some.

One of the most powerful Benedictine monasteries was that of Cluny which dated back to 909. It stood on Burgundian soil, the land having been granted by the Duke of Aquitaine. From a fairly humble beginning, Cluny soon grew rich and powerful. It spawned many daughter houses, some of which became extremely famous in their own right. The abbey at Cluny was grand, opulent and unbelievably wealthy. However, to suggest that it had, by the late eleventh century, become totally corrupt would be a misreading of the situation. Tolerance, charity and learning seem always to have remained at the heart of the ideal.

One of the greatest leaders at Cluny, Peter the Venerable, went so far as to have the Koran translated into Latin, and Cluny even eventually offered a safe retreat and home to Peter Abelard who had been savagely attacked and defeated by other monastic bodies for flying in the face of orthodox thinking with his modern philosophies.

It wasn't so much the "ideals" of Cluny that dissatisfied some of its youngest and most earnest brothers as the misinterpretation (in their eyes) of the sort of life originally envisaged for monks by St Benedict. Cluny had always given over most of the time of its monks to church services, and this was certainly a far cry from the later Cistercian abbeys where every one shared in hard manual work. Exactly how far St Benedict had intended brothers to go in the direction of physical labour is difficult to ascertain, but it is likely that he intended something half-way between Cluniac abstinence from secular duties and the ultimate Cistercian obsession with the field and the shearing knife.

There were many reformers who eventually left Cluny to seek a more austere form of monasticism, but the one who is most relevant to our story at this point was a volatile, erratic, but nevertheless sincere individual by the name of Robert de Molesmes. Robert was born in old Burgundy (Champagne to be precise) around 1028. He came to monasticism in an abbey very near to Troyes, the name of which was Montier-la-Celle. Such was his intelligence and the nature of his character that by the age of twenty-six he was already prior there. Doubtless the time he spent at Montier-la-Celle would have brought him into contact with some of the notables of Troyes, and almost certainly with the Counts of Champagne who would have known the abbey well.

Robert seems always to have been bad at toeing the Cluniac party line for although we was awarded the rank of abbot of another affiliated abbey, St-Michel Tonnerre, a couple of years later he was demoted and went back to Montier as a choir monk. In the year 1074 Robert set off again, this time with a band of fellow monks, in order to found the new abbey of Molesmes on land granted to him by Hugh de Maligny. Molesmes proved to be far more successful than Robert had anticipated and eventually he became weary with the degree of management necessary to cope with the funds and recruits flooding into the abbey. As a result, for a short while he instituted a hermitage elsewhere. Once again drawn back to Molesmes, Robert became the focal point of a split within the monks there, between those holding his own radical views and brothers dedicated to the original ideals of Cluny.

Dissatisfied with how things had been run, and weary of the turmoil within Molesmes, a group of the original hermits left to form an abbey of their own high in the Alps. The new hermitage, St Jean d'Aulps, held as part of its charter that the strict intention of the monks was to adhere rigorously to the tenets of St Benedict's Rule – to the exclusion of any other rule or doctrine. This new sub-order had the blessing of Abbot Rand and its very charter was drawn up by Stephen Harding, Robert's secretary and a man who would become important to the Cistercian order in his own right as we shall examine in due course.

Later, in 1097, matters at Molesmes came to a head. Robert received the grant of some land south of Dijon and with a small band of brothers he travelled there to found the mother house of all the later Cistercian monasteries, Citeaux. The land so generously donated to Abbot Robert for his new abbey was on Burgundian land. According to the *Exordium Parvum,* a document probably written by Stephen Harding, this land was owned by the Viscount Renard de Beaune who was urged by Odo, the Duke of Burgundy to donate it to Robert. Odo had a great deal of respect and admiration for Robert of Molesmes and this granting of Burgundian land to the Cistercian order would not be the last time Burgundian nobles would rally to the cause.

The abbey of Citeaux was dedicated in 1098 but Robert was not there for long. The sponsors and many of the monks of

Molesmes begged him to return; a request that he could no longer ignore once the local church authorities ordered him to do so. He left the new abbey of Citeaux in the hands of his second-in-command, Alberic, and under the equally admirable care of the man who had been for some years his secretary, a pious and quite brilliant Englishman by the name of Stephen Harding.

Stephen Harding was born of a wealthy Anglo-Saxon family and was educated in the abbey of Sherborne in Dorset, England. The year after the Battle of Hastings, 1067, Stephen set off on his travels and he never returned to England again. Exactly where he went during the next two or three years is a matter of conjecture. He certainly travelled to Rome and according to descendants of his family, quite possibly to Jerusalem. After this he spent some time in Paris, but he eventually found himself at Molesmes where the charismatic style and revolutionary ideas of Robert inspired in him a zeal for monastic reform that he would never abandon.

Upon the death of Alberic in 1109, Stephen Harding was nominated as abbott of Citeaux, and it is to this man that the ultimate order owes its initial debt. Stephen Harding was a great administrator, a patient and careful abbot and a great friend to the Burgundian and Champagne aristocracy. Under the careful guidance of Abbot Stephen, the Cistercian ideal began to take shape. The brothers chose a white habit, meant to symbolize purity. The original garb was probably more of a "dirty" grey untreated wool, but the monks soon began to bleach their habits and this is the same colour worn by Cistercian brothers to the present day. This was a stark departure from the black habits worn by the Benedictine and Cluniac monks, and was probably a reflection of the new found purity and adherence to the Benedictine ideal. We cannot help but draw a comparison between the white vestments adopted by Harding and those worn by the Essenes of Qumran, a group which figures prominently in our story.

From the very outset, the Cistercian ideal was one of unremitting work and prayer. So dedicated were the Cistercians to this ideal that the very motto of the order became, "*Ora et Labora*" or in English, "Pray and Work". It was suggested that the whole idea was based on St Benedict's rule, but it differed from the usual interpretation of Benedict's path in several respects.

First and foremost, the Cistercians adopted a radically new way of running their abbeys. They wanted to create their institutions in very remote places, "deserts" as they themselves said. This enforced a high degree of self-sufficiency which of course meant farming and gardening. To take on wage-earning locals to care for their animals and crops ran absolutely counter to the original Cistercian precepts so they instituted a two-tier form of brotherhood. Firstly there were choir monks, most of whom were ordained priests, who sang the services and then there were the lay brothers, who were less involved in matters of the mass but who were still monks who held binding vows.

This was a very attractive system because it meant that even the sons of lowly peasant stock could now embark upon the monastic life. When seen through modern eyes this way of life chosen by the first Cistercian lay brothers may seem rather odd, but we must put it in the context of the period of medieval Europe. In an era when an individual might not know where his next meal was coming from or if there would be enough wood for warmth in the winter, Cistercian laity offered a roof over one's head and a meal in the belly. A man might have to attend church a little more than normal, but that was a small price to pay for the security of existence offered by the Cistercian umbrella.

Lay brothers were not allowed to be ordained and to a great extent they lived a life apart from the true choir monks. Yet for all, they were an important part of the monastery and were not expected to work any harder than the choir monks. In fact the reverse was often true because the choir monks engaged in the same sort of manual labour as the lay brothers and were encouraged to offer an example by diligent concentration to the task in hand, whatever that may be. This was a period when the population of western Europe was on the increase. If we take this fact, together with the precarious nature of trying to earn a living outside of the monastery walls and the great rise in popular apocalyptical religion, it is easy to see that the Cistercians were not short of willing volunteers, for the positions of either choir or lay monks.

Another departure from the Cluniac tradition came with the actual look of the abbey and its attendant buildings. Everything was done to give the impression of absolute simplicity. Of course, in the earliest stages the monks of Citeaux were living in humble wooden buildings, but as the institution grew more elaborate, stone structures became possible. With the passing of centuries, ideals changed, but the first Cistercian churches were Spartan indeed. Cistercian churches were often mere chapels, though cruciform buildings did soon emerge. They carried no side aisles, no iconography and in fact nothing but stark white paint. Cistercian altars were plain affairs with a simple wooded cross flanked by one iron candlestick or two when communion was being taken. No statues or tombs of any sort were originally allowed in the church, and the body of the building was often split into two, so that lay brothers could occupy their own part of the church during services. The mass was sung in the simplest form of Gregorian plain song and services were kept as free from complication as possible. The vestments of the offici-ating priest were not brightly coloured and the whole impres-sion would not have unduly shocked the sensibilities of the staunchest Calvinist from the seventeenth century. All the original Cistercian monks were absolute vegetarians despite the fact that they kept extensive herds of cattle and, particularly, flocks of sheep.

Every morning, not long into the day, the monks would meet in chapter. Here they would discuss the routines for the coming day, admit to any transgressions and receive appropriate punishment if necessary. It was also in chapter that much of the important democratic business of the monastery took place. The head of every Cistercian monastery was the abbot who was chosen by the full brothers in chapter. If an abbot died, the brothers would select a new one, either from amongst their own number or from a different Cistercian house.

What set Cistercianism apart from the various other forms of monastic life available to the willing aspirant at the time was its strongly cohesive nature. Citeaux eventually represented the roots of a gigantic and ever spreading tree. From it sprang daughter houses, and new abbeys were eventually also formed by them. The rules and regulations of the Cistercians, known as the *Carta Caritatis* or *Charter of Charity*, was penned in its original form by St Stephen himself around 1111, a mere decade after the formation of Citeaux. It represented the constitution of a truly democratic institution of a type virtually unknown at the time. As the institution grew so all abbots were instructed to travel at least once a year to the mother house of their own branch of the Cistercian tree, and also once each year to Citeaux which remained the administrative headquarters for the entire Cistercian order. In the other direction, abbots from Citeaux or from abbeys that had daughter houses of their own would travel regularly to inspect newer houses and report back on their findings. Even the head of the whole Cistercian movement, the abbot of Clairvaux, was elected by a conclave of other Cistercian abbots. He was as liable to sanction as any other abbot and could have been dismissed by them if necessary since the machinery to do so existed in the Cistercian order. In this respect Cistercianism resembled the governmental structure of Anglo-Saxon England which, although not so democratic, had such principles at its heart. Under Anglo-Saxon rule all villagers were entitled to attend local meetings, known as "Things", from which representatives were chosen to represent the interests of a village, or a number of villages, at a larger, regional meeting known as a "Wapentak". From here, democratically chosen representatives would attend meetings with the king and the powerful lords of the land. In this way, it might be suggested that the most humble peasant at least had some sort of say in the running of his country. It should be remembered that this was exactly the sort of system under which Stephen Harding, himself of Anglo-Saxon stock, had been raised.

Citeaux was run no differently than any other Cistercian abbey, except that the administrative expectations were greater in the case of the overall mother house. From the very start, the pattern for the foundation of a new monastery, of which there would eventually be many, was laid down by Stephen Harding.

The procedure was invariably the same. When a particular abbey grew large enough, a group of monks would seek out new land (the wilder and more remote the better) and would then ask permission of the local landowner to place an abbey there. The Cistercians were very rarely refused. Not only did it confer a degree of "sanctity" upon a landowner to have a Cistercian monastery on his land, but also the monks actively improved what was, initially, unusable land.

At what stage the Cistercian began to specialize in sheep-rearing is difficult to say, but it is likely to have been almost immediately. This practice became most pronounced and especially profitable in the northern English abbeys, but it certainly took place at Citeaux and elsewhere in France as well.

Above all, St Stephen Harding's *Charter of Charity* was not only a prescription for the founding of daughter houses, but to some extent a code for Cistercian living. It was constructed very carefully and left no doubt or ambiguity in the mind of any prospective brother concerning what was expected of him. The six simple pages of Latin text that comprise this document, while outlining the code of conduct for the brethren, really wasn't anything new, as the Benedictine Rule that the Cistercians vowed to follow had previously outlined these aspects of monastic life. What is remarkable and revolutionary in Harding's *Carta Caritatis* is the infrastructure of the very order; the interconnectedness of all sister houses with the mother house of Citeaux. It seems that every contingency had been planned for – from the visitation of a brother abbot to what would happen if the abbot of Citeaux became corrupt. Chapter twelve of the document clearly outlines the democratic nature of Cistercianism, which was quite revolutionary in an age of Carolingian feudalism:

> If it happen (which may Heaven forfend) that the abbots of our Order learn that the abbot of Citeaux becomes cold in the practice of his duties and departs from the observance of the holy rule and constitutions, the four abbots of La Ferté, Potingny, Clairvaux and Morimond, shall, in the name of all the other abbots, admonish him to the fourth time, that he may correct himself and others. But if he prove incorrigible, then they must diligently carry out the instructions which we have given concerning the deposition of abbots, with this proviso: if he does not abdicate of his own accord, they can neither depose him, nor pronounce against him anathema unless in General Chapter. But if it would be too long to wait for that, they must proceed with their censures in an assembly of abbots who have been taken from the filiation of Citeaux, with others summoned for the occasion.

It is often wrongly stated by historians that the abbey of Citeaux virtually collapsed at the time Robert of Molesmes returned to his old responsibilities. In fact this is far from being the truth. Slowly at first, but very surely, the foundation flourished, having gained another completely new abbey to add to its own success before Bernard of Clairvaux and his family appeared on the scene.

On balance, we are inclined to suspect that the Burgundian Salt Line families almost certainly had a hand in the creation of the Cistercian order. There are several reasons why this is probably the case, not least of all the location deliberately chosen for the first abbey of Citeaux.

The abbey was carefully located at a longitude of exactly 51 degrees 1 minute east of Greenwich (although this refers to modern terminology which was irrelevant in the twelfth

century). This places Citeaux firmly on one of the longitudinal
Salt Lines first recognized and rediscovered by Xavier
Guichard (see chapter 2). Of course this state of affairs could be
a coincidence, but bearing in mind all the other Salt Line
evidence that we will be presenting, it seems very unlikely. One
of the possible etymologies of the word Citeaux is presented by
Stephen Tobin in his book, *The Cistercians*. According to
Tobin, Citeaux was the French translation for the Latin word
"*Cistercium*", which in itself was an abbreviation of the phrase
"*Cis tertium lapidem miliarium*" or "Just this side of the third
mile stone". This could be, as Tobin suggests, an old Roman
marker or perhaps an indication that those responsible for the
creation of the new abbey and the new monastic movement
were in possession of an intricate knowledge of Salt Line topog-
raphy. An alternative derivation might have something to do
with "Cisterns", an allusion to the Essene with which we shall
deal further presently.

It also seems most likely to us that many of the options
chosen by the first Cistercians regarding clothing, lifestyle and
the fundamental rules of their order were something much more
than mere adaptations of Benedictine norms. We hope these
matters will become self evident as our story proceeds though it
is only fair to admit that we cannot conclusively prove that the
Cistercian movement was created by the Burgundian Salt Line
families, rather than simply being used by them. Either way,
matters certainly came to a head in 1113 when thirty individuals, all from the same family, came together to the gates of
Citeaux, declaring themselves determined to join the order.

Though Citeaux was surviving fairly well, it probably did not
have many monks at the time since it had fostered a daughter
house very recently. The influx of new recruits, all members of
the powerful Burgundian Fontaine family who were based on
the Salt Line location of Fontaine immediately north of Dijon,
surely represents a deliberate attempt to take over the order at a
very crucial stage in its development.

At the head of this band of new recruits was a small but

earnest man of twenty-three years. His name was Bernard and he was a youngest son of the Fontaine family. Long and exaggerated stories came to be told concerning the manner by which he had begged, bullied and coerced so many relatives and friends into entering the monastery with him. We are inclined to believe that this was probably not the case and that the whole matter was a carefully stage-managed coup which assured Bernard in particular of a meteoric rise within the infant order.

The generally accepted story surrounding Bernard's life prior to entering Citeaux is not based on reliable, firsthand accounts. Any historian practised at studying descriptions of saints' lives learns quickly to read between the lines. Most of these accounts were put together in the years after the saint's death and the same sort of themes occur time and again. For example, we are both more than familiar with the account of a precious cloak being given to a particular saint by some king or noble, which is then torn in half and the pieces given to the poor. This story is so frequent in the lives of the saints that we marvel at the fact that any garment remained in one piece during the Middle Ages. This is only one small example of repeating themes, most of which seem to have been included in order to bolster a particular individual's right to sainthood.

The story of St Bernard is no exception in this regard, in fact it is one of the best examples of "retrospective justification for canonization" imaginable. As a result, it is difficult to read the account of his early life with anything other than a very sceptical attitude. Nevertheless, there are certain aspects of the tale that are probably true. Bernard seems to have shown himself to be of quite startling capabilities and intellect, even as early as his seventh year when his education commenced. Even at this stage, he was quiet and serious, but obviously a born leader. He was the third son of his family and seems to have had a particular regard for his mother. This part of the story is almost certain to be true if only because such an observation was rarely made of individuals at a time when fathers, rather than mothers, would have been the obvious male role model.

We know that Bernard's mother died while he was still fairly young, and that this had a tremendous bearing on his life. Bernard was first, last and middle, a Christian mystic, though how far this took him from the orthodox Christianity of his time we will presently see. His absolute veneration for the Christian Virgin Mary is often attributed to his special regard for a mother he lost before he really had chance to know her. However, if the stories relating to his life are to be believed, his visions of the Virgin started when he was a mere three years old. We have a very different explanation of St Bernard's reverence for the feminine. It is directly related to his family connections, together with the rich and ancient heritage of which his family was a part.

St Bernard and his family quickly settled into the routine of Citeaux. Clearly the influx of so many new recruits made it possible for a more rapid expansion to take place than might otherwise have been envisaged. Two years later in 1115, so the story goes, Hugh, Count of Champagne offered a tract of land not far from Troyes for the foundation of a new Cistercian abbey. Bernard was only twenty-five years of age and had been a monk for just over two years and yet, against all the odds, he was chosen to be abbot of the new establishment, which he called Clairvaux. Despite his inexperience and that fact that there must have been more worthy monks present at Citeaux (at least in terms of the number of years served with the order), Bernard found himself a few miles from Troyes, and in the selfsame year important events that had recently been discussed at the palace in Troyes were coming to fruition. One of the men involved in these discussions was André de Montbard, a close ally of Count Hugh and a man who was to be one of the first Templar knights. André was Bernard's own uncle on the maternal side of the family. Bernard's family were blood-tied with that of Count Hugh and there may also have been a kin-tie with Hugh de Payens, first grand master of the Templars.

It seems almost unnecessary to point out that Bernard's new abbey of Clairvaux occupied a location on a latitudinal Salt Line, and that its positioning was also highly significant in terms of megalithic mathematics and geometry for other reasons. Historians have often suggested that Bernard founding a new abbey on the doorstep of the Champagne court, particularly bearing in mind that this was made possible by the Count of Champagne who himself became a member of the Knights Templar, was probably no coincidence. Not only are we inclined to agree with this point of view, but would go as far as to suggest that the foundation of Clarivaux was merely another deliberate move on the part of a group of people whose agenda was well planned, but whose motives have been a mystery until now.

Chapter 8

The Mellifluous Doctor

There have been numerous attempts by theologians and historians alike to fully understand and explain the motivations of St Bernard of Clairvaux. Although he certainly ranks as one of the most influential people who ever lived in western Europe, and despite the fact that he wrote extensively during his own lifetime, the wealth of information left to us does nothing to explain the obvious "hidden agenda" in many of his actions. As our research has advanced we have become more and more convinced that St Bernard was simply one member of a network of individuals who were working to a particular set of imperatives, many of which may have first been set in motion generations before he was born.

We have observed that Bernard was part of a wider family that was destined to play an important part in the story of Europe and the Levant in the years immediately after the First Crusade. In addition we have suggested that many of the members of this family and people with whom he regularly mixed had been born on Salt Lines or else held land in such locations. This is certainly true in the case of Hugh Count of Champagne, Hugh Count of Dijon and the general of the First Crusade, Godfroi de Bouillon, together with his brother

Baudoin. In addition, we cannot forget André de Montbard, Bernard's uncle, or Hugh de Payens, who will come to play a bigger part in our story presently.

But what of Bernard's own Salt Line credentials? Bernard's birthplace was Fountaine de Dijon, which is located immediately north of the city of Dijon on the same longitudinal Salt Line that passes through the city and which also runs very close to the new Cistercian foundation of Citeaux. So, we can say that Bernard was not only born on a Salt Line location, but that he chose to enter a Salt Line monastery too. Two years later he became abbot of Clairvaux, this time on a latitudinal Salt Line location between Langres and Troyes. Bernard was destined, despite his many travels, to die at his beloved Clairvaux, where he was buried. But even this is not the extent of his involvement with Salt Lines, which remained relevant even after his death.

With the arrival of the French Revolution, the golden reliquary containing the skull of St Bernard was melted down for coinage. Representatives of the Strict Order of Cistercianism, the Trappists, rescued St Bernard's skull and carried it for safety to Switzerland. Eventually it was deemed safe to bring this most precious relic back to France. But the skull never went back to Clairvaux; on the contrary, it was placed with great reverence in the longitudinal Salt Line city of Troyes where it resides to this day in the treasury of Troyes cathedral.

It is important to point out to our reader at this juncture that according to the research and observations of Xavier Guichard the longitudinal and latitudinal Salt Lines are mathematical phenomena and, as such, they fall across the landscape where they must. It is therefore the case that latitudinal Salt Lines occur every 111 kilometres apart, whilst longitudinal ones vary according to the latitudes across which they are measured. As a general rule of thumb, in the latitudes of the broader area of Burgundy the Salt Lines of longitude are around 80 kilometres apart. Even someone who had grave doubts about the validity of Guichard's observations would surely have to admit that if the Salt Lines are nonexistent, we are looking at a truly fantastic series of coincidences, even when dealing with the life of St Bernard in isolation.

It is not our intention here to try and itemize what the Salt Lines might actually "be". Arguments as to their creation in Bronze Age times, or alternatively the concept that they may have an origin relating to the physics of the planet upon which we live and the solar system of which it is part, belong elsewhere. In fact they are being pursued by other agencies as we write these words. For now, we content ourselves with observations and note the connections between specific characters that were of Salt Line origin and who shared kinship and other ties during the period in question.

St Bernard of Clairvaux is one such character. It was the knowledge of the strong Salt Line associations of his life that first marked him out as a man worthy of greater study, and what we learned only strengthened our belief that his life and mission represented part of something much bigger than his own sense of calling or even some of his proffered beliefs.

St Bernard took up the reins of Clairvaux in 1118 whilst still a very young man. Almost immediately he began to gain a reputation for himself within the Catholic Church as a whole. As we have seen, St Bernard was a mystic and never attempted to disguise the fact. Many incidents added to his supposed reverence for Christian mysticism. Not least amongst these was a happening that took place in the cathedral at Chalon when he was still a very young monk. Bernard was officiating at mass in the cathedral when he claimed that the statue of the Virgin Mary, above the altar, came to life. Speaking of the incident later, he claimed that the Virgin had put her hand to her breast and that drops of milk from the breast had dripped into his open mouth.

We would probably see such a reported event these days in strictly Freudian terms and some experts have associated it with the fact that Bernard lost his mother while he was very young and that this had a great bearing on his psychological makeup subsequently. We are not so sure of this interpretation, but for whatever reason this supposed happening is said to have altered St Bernard's view of the Virgin Mary ever after. Even the psychological explanation is probably wide of the mark because Bernard is also supposed to have seen a vision of the Virgin Mary as early as three years of age, whilst his mother did not die until he was seventeen. In our comprehension, whether or not the saintly little man from Dijon actually did undergo a mystical happening, his belief in the phenomenon led him to a course of action entirely in keeping with what we have come to expect of the Burgundian Salt Line families.

As Bernard of Clairvaux's power and influence grew, he made it his business to become a "pope maker". The man in question was Gregorio Papareschi, whose adopted name as pope was Innocent II. The story of Innocent II's rise to the rank of undisputed pope is interesting if only because it shows the depth of support that the Burgundian Salt Line families actually had in certain important places and within the ruling families of Europe. Beyond this, it demonstrates the skill with which they were able to set one faction against another in order to achieve their own peculiar objectives.

Bernard was thirty years of age when Pope Honorius II died on 13 February 1130, and he was already deeply respected for his learning and piety. Bernard's choice for the papacy was Gregorio Papareschi, who initially had only a minority of support from the cardinals. Although Papareschi was almost immediately declared pope, there was another and more popular contender. This man was Pietro Pierleoni, who is now referred to as the anti-Pope Anacletus II. Some historians of the Church still claim that Anacletus actually had more right to the Vatican, but he lacked the very powerful support that Bernard of Clairvaux was able to cull for Innocent II.

We shall discuss presently exactly why Innocent was Bernard's choice, but Bernard went to extraordinary lengths to support him. In a way, this was strange because Anacletus II had been trained in Cluny, the monastery from which ultimately

Citeaux, Clairvaux and in fact the whole Cistercian order had derived. Nevertheless, Bernard immediately put pressure on all the agencies he knew to support Papareschi, by now known as Innocent II. A particular ally proved to be Norbert, Archbishop of Magdeberg, himself a deeply pious monk from an order very similar to the Cistercians. Norbert, later St Norbert, was a man close to the heart of Lothair, king of Germany, and he and Bernard persuaded Lothair to support Innocent in the struggle for the papacy. As a result, Lothair invaded Italy and personally placed Innocent II on the throne of the Vatican. Bernard had also managed to bring the French Church round to his way of thinking, together with Henry I of England. Bernard had travelled many thousands of kilometres and preached hundreds of sermons in his efforts to have Innocent declared the true pope. It is obvious that he must have felt extremely committed to the cause of this man and yet there is very little to indicate that Anacletus II would have made a particularly bad pope.

Historians have suggested that the main thrust of Bernard's support for Innocent lay in the new pontiff's attitude toward Church power. It was a basic tenant of the feudal system (or at least accepted as such by many feudal monarchs) that kings and wealthy landowners should choose the clergy for the areas over which they had sway. Bernard was strictly opposed to this notion. Some of the reasons for his opposition have already been itemized. At heart, Bernard of Clairvaux was a believer in the old Roman and Celtic Church which had ruled its own affairs, quite immune from interference from the king or his vassal lords. This was the Burgundian and Merovingian way, and the Salt Line families appear never to have swayed from a belief in extremely old forms of Christianity.

Pope Innocent II showed his intention, from the word go, of doing everything within his power to oppose the imposition of the State's will over Church business. Anacletus was more giving with this regard, or at the very least flexible concerning the issue. Such apparent ambivalence was simply not enough for Bernard of Clairvaux who had his own very definite reasons for keeping the affairs of Church and State as separate as possible.

This issue alone might have been enough to suggest that Bernard would naturally support Innocent II and that he would do all in his power to raise enthusiasm for the man elsewhere, but the reign of Innocent proved that there was much more to it than this. Not that Bernard was beyond reproaching the pope he had created if it proved necessary to do so. He once wrote to Innocent in the following terms:

> There is but one opinion among all the faithful shepherds among us, namely, that justice is vanishing in the Church, that the power of the keys is gone, that episcopal authority is altogether turning rotten, while not a bishop is able to avenge the wrongs done to God, nor is allowed to punish any misdeeds whatever, not even in his own diocese (*parochia*). And the cause of this they put down to you and the Roman Court.

Among the first actions undertaken by Innocent II upon receiving more or less universal acclaim as the true pope, were his speeches relating to much earlier Christian edicts regarding the Virgin Mary. Mary had always held a special place in the hearts of Christian devotees, but in the Western Church at least her actual position within the Christian hierarchy was somewhat ambiguous. Innocent II took care of this matter at a stroke. Supporting decisions that had been made in Ephesus centuries before, Innocent openly declared the Virgin Mary to be considered (as she already was in the East) "the Mother of God" and "Queen of Heaven".

This point of view is still hard for some Christian thinkers to reconcile with the very conception of what "godhead" represents. There are still many attempts within Catholic circles to try and explain what these terms actually mean. In non-Arian Christian circles, it was ultimately decided that Jesus was essentially "of the same substance" as God, and was therefore indivisible from God.

If Mary was the mother of Jesus, it therefore followed that she must be the mother of God. But this point of view can be seen as deeply contentious because it might be suggested that in order to be the mother of God, Mary would have had to predate God. The whole situation is further complicated by her being granted the title "Queen of Heaven". Surely in Christian thinking, God is the "King of Heaven" and so the inferred relationship between God and Mary is somewhat open to question.

Almost everything that happened subsequently with regard to the Cistercians, and the Templars, leads us to believe that Bernard had been in a position to put pressure on the new pope to make such declarations regarding the Virgin Mary, and that he had a very good reason for doing so. Of course, Bernard could be expected to be a staunch supporter of the Virgin since every Cistercian monastery was dedicated to her name and indeed she would be the patroness of the Templar order too. But, if our general assumptions are correct, this elevation of the Virgin was yet another careful and calculated step towards eventually usurping the power of the established Church altogether. At the very least, it could be seen in feudal and Vatican terms as being a revisionist policy and many raised eyebrows across Western Christianity must have resulted.

It is interesting to note that the "Assumption" of Mary, i.e. the belief that her body was taken up into heaven at the time of her passing from earthly life, was not declared to be Christian dogma until 1950. Even this may be seen as an attempt by the Vatican to quell some of the apparent ambiguity regarding her "special status". The inference that she was "assumed into Heaven" appears to give greater credence to her full humanity and detracts from the divine associations of her rank as "Mother of God" and "Queen of Heaven". It is also strange to relate that although Bernard became one of the staunchest supporters of Mary, he would never accept the idea of her immaculate conception which presupposes that she was absolutely sinless from the time of her conception and therefore the only suitable vessel for the representation of God that Jesus was meant to be.

Of course, it is possible that Innocent II was fully in accord with Bernard's own beliefs regarding Mary. However, it is equally likely that, in the case of Innocent, Bernard's wishes regarding the Virgin would have seemed modest in return for guaranteeing him the Vatican. Innocent almost certainly had no idea what the Burgundian Salt Line family was planning.

Innocent II would not be the only pope that Bernard virtually controlled. Some years later, in 1145, Bernardo Paganelli became pope as Eugene III. His election was sudden, dramatic and quite unexpected. Even more than Innocent II, Paganelli appears to have been Bernard's man, as Bernard had personally trained him as a novice at the abbey of Clairvaux!

At a personal level, Bernard of Clairvaux appeared to be amongst the holiest and best sons of the Roman Catholic Church. He was pious, charitable, caring and, apparently, a willing follower of the Church party line. Of course, this is a little like suggesting that the dictator of a particular country personifies all the laudable virtues imaginable when these virtues are being extolled by the information machine controlled by the dictator himself. During the whole of his adult life Bernard held the Church in the palm of his hand. He rarely made a wrong move and was extremely careful not to publicly quarrel with anyone who might be in a position to undermine his power. There are two edges to most swords and even contemporaries admitted that Bernard could be irascible, argumentative and headstrong, but he had such powerful friends that nobody with any sense would have openly doubted his word or poured scorn on his judgement.

It is not our intention to give the impression that Bernard of Clairvaux was devoid of the natural gifts and virtues with which his memory is replete. On the contrary, he was an able leader, an astute politician, a charismatic preacher and writer, and in most respects he personified a man of deep and enduring belief. As far as this last quality is concerned, we remain determined that what he believed and what he purported to believe were frequently two different things.

In his personal life, Bernard was abstemious and exact. He adhered absolutely to the Cistercian way of simplicity and extolled its virtues for the whole of his life. He kept no mistress (which was not universally the case, even for high Church officers during this period) and indeed would have been horrified at the contemplation of even occupying a seat that had recently supported a female rump. However, this did nothing to deter his almost fanatical zeal for the "feminine" within his chosen faith. Bernard had been born in Fontaine, just a kilometre of two from the old pagan site of "Is", which had been dedicated since time out of mind to a female deity that the Romans had clearly identified with the Egyptian goddess Isis. Many of the cathedrals visited and favoured by Bernard were centres of the Black Madonna cult. Statues of the Virgin were held in these cathedrals and venerated in their own right. Some of the statues were contemporary with Bernard's own period, but the majority had probably existed long before Christianity came to western Europe.

The French researcher Louis Charpentier, in his book *The Mysteries of Chartres Cathedral*, draws an interesting parallel between many of the French churches that Bernard would have known well and visited often. He claims that place names such as Chartres, Troyes and Rhiems would originally have been thought of as "Chart Is", "Troy Is" and "Rhiem Is", in which the suffix of the name set these places apart as being sacred to the very same feminine deity for whom Bernard's own local sanctuary of "Is" was named. The Burgundians, originally coming from the island of Bornholm, were of a race to whom the thought of a masculine deity without a feminine element to balance it would have been unthinkable. And if we look for a moment at the situation regarding the Virgin Mary, as Bernard left it, we can immediately recognize Bernard's desire to recreate something that was already as old as time in the region where he lived.

We know from our research into the Minoan culture that the basic religious beliefs of this culture revolved around a perpetual goddess, personified as the Earth itself and celebrated through the passing of the seasons. To this goddess was born a boy child, who was known as the "Young God". He grew to maturity and became the consort of the goddess, and was then known as the "Old God". In time he would die, leaving the goddess to bear a child who would become the Young God once more.

Mary, when seen as both the "Mother of God" and also the "Queen of Heaven", seems to perpetuate the Minoan goddess role perfectly. The religious beliefs of Minoan Crete were almost certainly paralleled by those in the far west of Europe during the megalithic period. These were the selfsame people who had given birth to the Burgundians when their home was still Bornholm. We have seen already that the island is replete with megalithic monuments.

Further evidence for Bernard's personal respect for a feminine aspect to godhead comes from his virtual obsession with a book of the Bible known as Solomon's Song of Songs. This is one of the strangest parts of the Jewish and Christian Old Testament, and at base owes little to Judaism in its present, orthodox sense. Solomon's Song of Songs represents a series of extremely beautiful, but also deeply erotic, verses primarily concerning a conversation between a bride and a bridegroom. Bernard wrote many sermons based upon the Song of Songs. Generally, he drew a parallel between the Church and the bride whilst he considered Jesus to be the bridegroom.

Considering Bernard's special reverence for King Solomon, perhaps it isn't surprising that he should take such pleasure in a work that the Jewish king is said to have personally composed. It is doubtful to us, however, that St Bernard's interest in this work was ever quite what it appeared to be. Some light was thrown on this fact by the authors Lynne Picknett and Clive Prince who demonstrated in their book *The Templar Revelation* that Solomon's Song of Songs is, in reality, an almost perfect translation of an Egyptian wedding rite dedicated to none other than the goddess Isis.

At writing, Bernard excelled, though it is a wonder that so many documents, sermons, letters and even virtual books were ever composed for he was rarely in one place for more than a few months at a time. Almost any cause relevant to the Church of his day was of interest to the little man from Dijon, despite the fact that he suffered from fairly chronic ill health almost from the time of his monastic vows. And as if Christian business was not enough to keep this irrepressible man occupied, he also made it his business, as we have previously observed, to keep an eye on the Jewish communities within France too.

Bernard was sent to the south of France in 1145 in order to try and convert the heretic Cathar to a more orthodox form of Christianity. The Cathar had strange beliefs for they held to the conviction that all of material life must be essentially evil, which threw some doubt on their belief in Jesus as the Christ and the Son of God. Some hundred years after St Bernard's death, these generally peaceful people were slaughtered in their tens of thousands in the Albigensian Crusades, but Bernard would never have condoned such action. Despite his ruthless streak, especially when dealing with opponents, it does seem to have been the case that Bernard could see good, and indeed "God", in almost anyone. Upon returning from southern France, where he achieved almost no success in converting the Cathar, he nevertheless declared them to be amongst the most "Godly" people he had ever met.

By the standards of his day, Bernard had received a fairly liberal education, for in addition to religion he had been taught much about Greek Philosophy and had personally studied a number of works that would, at some stage, be burned as deeply offensive to the Church. Despite his studies, he appeared to retain a point of view that revered the essence of "faith" rather than the overuse of logic. It was upon this premise that he was forced to cross swords with Peter Abelard. Abelard was, by the standards of his times, a revolutionary thinker, deeply committed to rationalism and the extreme exaltation of human reason. Bernard would have none of this and preferred instead to stick to his own certitude of faith.

Abelard refused to temper his style, or his ideas, and Bernard grew more and more agitated with the damage he thought was being done. In the end, and probably contrary to his natural inclination, Bernard attacked Abelard publicly with all the weight that his elevated position within the Church allowed. The result was that Peter Abelard was all but destroyed and was forced to retire to the ultimate seclusion of one of Cluny's smaller daughter houses.

We have spent a great deal of time subjecting St Bernard's actions to the most minute scrutiny we can employ and for some time we remained puzzled by the attacks he made on Peter Abelard, which seem to fly in the face of what we see as the main springboard of thinking employed by the Burgundian Salt Line fraternity. Both the Cistercians and the Templars used forms of democracy and there is much evidence to show that the Burgundian Salt Line confederacy was opposed to the overly strict rule of the Roman Catholic Church and to the very substance of feudalism. We are left with the impression that this uncharacteristic outburst on the part of St Bernard may well have been brought about as a result of his concern that what Abelard was suggesting was "too much, too soon". These matters were taking place at a time when the Salt Line fraternity desperately needed the cohesion and power of the Roman Catholic Church which it fully intended to turn to its own ends. If radical free-thinkers such as Peter Abelard were allowed to knock the foundations out from under the Church, there was a strong chance that they would also destroy Bernard's plans and those of the agencies he represented. However, typical of the sort of man he was, Bernard ensured that he was eventually reconciled with Abelard, a man who had been far from complimentary about Bernard and for whom Bernard himself might have been expected to retain a particular disdain.

Although Clairvaux was in every sense a daughter house of Citeaux, St Bernard ruled as chief star in his own firmament. He was never abbot of Citeaux and probably never wished to be, though it is a fact that those who held that office during his lifetime were perpetually eclipsed by his light. Cistercianism expanded at a truly phenomenal rate while Bernard lived, and his own abbey of Clairvaux inspired a large number of daughter houses of its own. But Bernard remained a simple soul, despite the fact that he so skilfully supervised the meteoric rise of his chosen order. He had many friends amongst monks from overseas, especially Saxons such as his mentor Stephen Harding, but in particular Celtic, Culdean-inspired brothers such as St Malachy. Malachy, an Irish monk and now also a saint, eventually died in the arms of St Bernard and was buried at Clairvaux. His skull and thighbone shares the precious and beautiful Merovingian reliquary that houses St Bernard's own skull in Troyes cathedral.

St Bernard's long and warm relationship with Malachy is a demonstration of his regard for the Celtic Culdean Church practices. Bernard lived in interesting times and was the chief representative of a powerful subculture within society which also sought a return to pre-Catholic values. Anyone doubting that St Bernard personally harboured Culdean motives only has to read his own words:

> Believe me, for I know, you will find something far greater
> in the woods than in books. Stones and trees will teach you
> that which you cannot learn from the masters.

This concept is carried through in St Bernard's own involvement in church architecture. He is often credited with the introduction of the "Gothic" movement. In this form of architecture, the force of gravity is seemingly confounded by the use of flying buttresses which, in taking the load from high walls and redistributing it, allow a cathedral or abbey to "leap" from the ground on which it stands. Tier on tier of pointed arches span pillars that leave one feeling that one is standing in the midst of a petrified forest. Great windows pour pure light into this "forest clearing" which Bernard wanted desperately to keep free of any sort of intrusive human creation that would serve to remove the "magic" from the geometrically derived expression of living nature. Remove the statuary, the complex screens, the ornate carving and the modern pews from any of the great cathedrals that bear testimony to the earliest flowering of Gothic genius and what remains is as pure, as stark and as fundamental as St Bernard would have personally wished it to be. Gothic structures are not raised "on the earth"; they are drawn up from it.

St Bernard of Clairvaux should be judged as one of the most remarkable men of whom we can reliably bear witness. At heart he was a true "pagan". Unfortunately this word has taken on many connotations that seem to leave it as an entirely inappropriate description for one of the acclaimed doctors of the Church. But in our conception, St Bernard would have retained his spiritual purity in any age and amongst any religious convention. In essence, he worked "within" Christian orthodoxy (up to a point), but he was never "of" it. He ranks with the likes of the much more modern Indian mystic, politician and religious leader Mahatma Gandhi. In fact, the similarities between the two men are legion. The only essential difference, apart from religious background, lies in the fact that in the case of Gandhi, no necessary deception hid his true motives from the world. Gandhi was willing to die for what he believed, but Bernard of Clairvaux could allow himself no such luxury, and had to be circumspect with the truth of his beliefs as a result.

We have much more to learn about this remarkable character and about the truly incredible events he helped to set in play. Those of us who find something to admire in the modern world owe that admiration, in great part, to this often sick and tired little man from the heart of Burgundy. He took Cistercianism, no more than a barely flourishing ideal when he joined the order, and made it into something the like of which the world had not previously seen and would never know again. And it is towards the day-to-day reality of that monastic ideal that we must now turn our attention.

Chapter 9

The Cistercian Monks

While it remains true that some branches of the rival Augustinian canons practised manual labours, the "severe" branches of this extremely popular order shunned physical toil with all the fervency of the Benedictines. Despite this one similarity, the two rival monastic institutions of Cistercian monks and Augustinian canons were diametrically opposed in other respects. Most noticeably, the Augustinian brothers lived alongside society, their monasteries tending to be placed in areas where there was a castle, village or town. By contrast, the Cistercians shunned society and sought refuge in the wilds, taking unusable land and turning it into virtual Gardens of Eden.

During the late years of the twelfth century, the prime source of income for the average monastic order was from tithes, rents, church profits and the various offices available at their altars. In this last regard, the Augustinians flourished, being located in populous areas for this very reason. For example, rich patrons would pay large amounts to have masses sung or spoken for the repose of their souls. At the time of their commencement the Cistercians refused to take part in such activities, viewing the entire business with scorn. This type of simony reeked of

Carolingian feudalism, a political expedient that the order had opposed from day one and, to some extent, throughout its existence.

The very fact that the Cistercians sought solitude in wild and untamed places may have led, in part, to the gradual demise of feudalism. In the period during which the Cistercian sister houses were beginning to dot the landscape of Europe, new farming land was in relatively short supply. Some years before English abbeys such as Fountains or Rievaulx had come into existence, William I of England, a king who was very fond of hunting, issued forest laws to ensure that an increase in farming did not slow down the rate of growth of the wild deer population. Many barons in England, Normandy and France concurred with William and would burn down the house of any man who made a clearing in the forest without their leave. They fervently believed that it was their God-given right as feudal lords to do what they wished with their own lands.

Into this deeply repressive world came the Cistercians with songbook in one hand and axe in the other. With seeming impunity they began to clear parts of the forests here and there, turning what was often marginal land into profitable acreage. Noting the success of the Cistercians, other monastic institutions began to follow suit but with one major difference. The Benedictines would build or attract a "bourg" or town around any new house they founded. From this area of commerce and habitation, the order would collect rents and thus grow rich from the labour of others. Lay lords and monarchs were quite capable of knowing a good thing when they saw it and soon began to follow the trend. For example, the Capetian king Louis VII made quite a name for himself by forming new towns or "*villeneuves*" around his estate in the twelfth century. Because good, productive farmland was scarce, clearing marginal land became popular. For this reason, colonization of these lands became a matter of competition among rival lords, and the only real incentive was to offer better terms and conditions to would-be settlers. Chief among the incentives offered by the landowners was a greater freedom of life generally. To the peasants, who had for generations been absolutely subservient to the landowners, the notion of paying rent and shrugging off some of the constraints of serfdom held great appeal. Instead of owing a complete duty to the landowner this new form of peasant could work hard to raise his own crops, paying a fair rent but retaining more of the products of his own labour. It is at this time that the expression "town air makes free" came into the English language.

So it can be seen that by accident or design the Cistercians were at least partly responsible for a freedom among European citizens not previously experienced and this in turn sprang from a zealous monastic need to escape the very society that they by virtue of their labours were helping to create. But there were penalties, too, for divorced from the normal sources of revenue upon which monastic houses had traditionally relied, how would the fledgling order survive?

Many observers must have thought that without the normal reliance on the collection plate the Cistercian order would certainly be doomed to failure. However, such was not to be the case and the order grew to seven daughter houses within the first two decades. After a period of fifty years, the institution had expanded at a phenomenal rate to over three hundred such houses scattered throughout much of Europe and beyond. And it has to be recognized that hard, physical toil was the key to this success.

As we have seen, the Cistercians only chose land that was a virtual wasteland. Indeed, the order would accept only full ownership of new land, never settling in areas where they would be required to pay rent. In most cases, the land was freely donated to the order and our research had shown that, in the earliest days of the Cistercian order, in virtually all cases these were sites donated by Burgundian Salt Line families. This was certainly the case with the first land donated to Robert of Molesmes, who was granted the land for Citeaux by Renard of Beaune, who in turn had been persuaded to make the gift by

Odo I, the Duke of Burgundy. When land became more difficult to find, the Cistercians adopted a new strategy. As the popularity of the order grew, the Cistercians simply looked for an area that suited their needs and became squatters. Few lords proved willing to throw such an esteemed order of holy men off their lands.

At first there was a definite pattern to the locations chosen. Alan's previous research had shown that most of the original Cistercian holdings were on Salt Lines. This, together with the Salt Line origination of so many of the characters concerned, seems to indicate that the Cistercian order, or at least its leaders, was in possession of knowledge of Salt Line geography. The positioning of Clairvaux in particular seems to indicate that they were also in possession of the relevant measuring systems.

Cistercians always chose land that was on or near to a river. The reasons for this choice should soon become evident. It has been claimed by many researchers, and especially by Stephen Tobin in his book *The Cistercians*, that the white monks alone amongst all the medieval monastic institutions built their churches in the knowledge of "Earth forces". This may seem to be a wholly New-Age assumption. However, as far as we can ascertain, pre-Christian Druidic teaching had followed the notion that underground streams and springs originated within the body of the Earth Mother Goddess. If this is the case, there is little wonder that Citeaux and all Cistercian churches that followed it were dedicated to the Virgin Mary, who we have shown replaced the role of Mother Goddess within the early Christian Trinity. The reader will recall that St Bernard fervently promoted Mary and insisted on the use of her titles as "Mother of God" and "Queen of Heaven". Whether the selection of sites served by a freshwater supply was merely a matter of spirituality, practicality or perhaps a little of both is a matter for conjecture. What remains a fact is that the Cistercians did choose such sites and, wherever possible, on the Salt Line locations mentioned earlier. But although the early Cistercians were men of vision and deep spiritual conviction, they were also realists, as the layout of their abbeys demonstrates wonderfully.

To visit almost any of the elegant and serene Cistercian abbey ruins of western Europe is an experience that is not easily forgotten, especially when one considers the period during which they were built. While conducting research for this book, we visited several of the largest and finest Cistercian abbeys and especially those in the north of England. We were not disappointed with any of them. The sheer scale and efficiency of design is still evident, even in those cases where little of the original fabric remains. From cloister to nave, and chapter house to reredorter, no space was wasted and each of the abbeys remains beautiful in its austere simplicity. Benedictine monasteries of the early twelfth century were opulent and ornate. By stark contrast, Cistercian monasteries were simplistic and plain. No stained-glass filled the great east window and no gold adorned the altars. These buildings of God were as simple in appearance as were the men who occupied their many rooms. But austerity does not preclude good function. It is still clear from the ruins available for examination that much thought went into the design of the abbeys. No matter where one travels within Europe, a consistency of purpose can be perceived. It might even be fair to suggest that a blind French monk could quite easily have found his way around an English Cistercian abbey. Even today, the mother house of Citeaux, still a working monastery, displays a similar pattern.

At the commencement of a new Cistercian foundation, twelve choir monks would arrive along with an abbot and a group of lay brethren. New abbeys were almost always settled by this grouping of thirteen monks. Some researchers hold that it was symbolic of Christ and the twelve apostles, while others contend that it was a representation of the twelve astrological signs and the sun. Whatever the truth of this matter, it was a pattern that remained intact throughout the larger part of the early and middle Cistercian adventure. It is interesting to note that the Knights Templar always elected a new grand master with the same arrangement, of twelve knights and a cleric.

The first procedure on newly acquired lands was to erect either a wooden or stone chapel as the monks were specifically bound to hold their daily services. Even beyond toil, devotion to God was the first order of business for the monks. Next on the agenda was to throw up some humble living quarters while a more systematic and permanent construction began. These were usually rudimentary and humble wooden structures designed for no other purpose than to provide the work crews with shelter. While the lay brothers were certainly the backbone of the labours, we have seen that the choir monks also pitched in with the tasks at hand, in keeping with the Cistercian motto *"Ora et Labora"*. As work progressed a small group of choir monks and unskilled lay brothers alone could not build the structure that would eventually grace the site. It is certain that skilled masons were employed by the order to assist in erecting the many structures that would form a new abbey. Any new house took a bare minimum of five years to establish properly, and so one of the first tasks had to be the provision of food.

Crops would be planted to provide food for the workforce of choir monks, lay brethren and hired hands. Agriculture was a form of endeavour in which the Cistercians excelled and it was the one that was ultimately to make the order so wealthy.

The first of the monastery buildings to be completed was the abbey church. The masons would start with the east end as all Cistercian abbeys were designed to face Jerusalem. Even in cases such as Rievaulx Abbey in Yorkshire where, because of the lay of the land, the abbey could not face east, it was referred to as the east or Ecclesiastical East. Cistercian abbey churches were of a cruciform shape, following the Benedictine plan, though with slight modifications. The Benedictine churches, which the Cistercians used as a model, had a rounded apse in the east whereas the Cistercians preferred square-ended churches. The probable reason for this is that the rounded apse served no real purpose save ornamentation and that was in direct opposition to the Cistercian style of architecture.

Stone arriving from the quarry, pre-cut and shaped, would be piled upon stones already placed, until scaffolding could be erected to assist in the raising of the church. Carpenters would be employed for this task, as well as to build the many wooden frames required to support the building of the vaulted arches used to support the buttresses and arches that held the roof. These buttresses were based on those created by the order in Burgundy. The roof would be built on the ground in sections and hoisted by primitive crane to be affixed piece by piece. It is a shame that in England these roofs no longer exist, most having been removed by Thomas Cromwell who was charged with the task of dissolving the monasteries by Henry VIII in the sixteenth century. The roofs were dismantled for the lead that had been used in their construction; lead which, in the main, had been mined and smelted by the Cistercians themselves.

The inside of a typical Cistercian church, such as that at Rievaulx in Yorkshire, consisted of three main portions; the nave, transepts and presbytery. The nave and side transepts of Rievaulx Abbey form what is one of the oldest extant Cistercian churches in Europe, and although the nave is all but ruined, a walk through it remains a delight. One can plainly perceive how beautiful this building was in its day; how the barrelled vaults carried the arches' profile back to the aisle walls. One of the first impressions is of the sheer height of the roof and it was rather appropriate that on the day we visited stonemasons were hammering away with mallet and chisel, a haunting reminder of what life in the monastery must have been like during the days when construction was taking place. The nave at Rievaulx, which consisted of nine bays, housed two separate churches: the lay brothers' choir as well as the monk's choir. This alone was massive by the standard of the day, but formed only a portion of the entire abbey church.

Around 1210, Rievaulx's new presbytery was constructed. It consisted of seven bays and was three storeys high. The eastern bay alone consisted of five chapels, one in each of the aisles and three in the centre. It is interesting that the three central chapels contained images of St John the Baptist, St John the Evangelist and the Virgin Mary – a very peculiar trinity, and one that will bear a further examination when we look further into the Knights Templar and the Freemasons, the latter of which retain a very high regard for the two St Johns in question.

Once the church proper was completed, the craftsman moved on to the choir monks' dormitory, lay brothers' quarters, chapter house, cloister and other areas of the abbey.

Of all the additional buildings of the Cistercian abbey, the chapter house deserves a closer look. The chapter house is so named because it was in this large room that the monks would gather daily to hear the reading of a chapter of the rule of St Benedict. Here, the business of the order was conducted and meetings held on a multitude of subjects. So important were these meetings that if a monk was tardy or absent, he was found, brought to the chapter house and beaten in front of his brethren. This form of corporal punishment is a stark contrast to our conception of monks as peace-loving hermits. However, it must be remembered that the Cistercians were essentially a military-style organization and have more in common, in many respects, with their brother order the Templars than to the Benedictines from whom they were descended. Such beatings were generally accepted as part of the lot of the Cistercian monk and, paradox-ically, were meted out as a result of the same democratic ground rules that lay at the heart of all Cistercian life. In any case, it is evident that they tended to be ritualistic rather than existing to offer any real pain. In other words, they were a psychological and spiritual deterrent to tardiness rather than a physical one.

The design of the Cistercian chapter house was more or less the same from abbey to abbey throughout Europe. It was a rectangular structure with a rounded apse in the east end, similar in design to the apse found in the east end of Benedictine churches. Entrance to the meeting room was from the cloister where the monks gathered to study, read and wash before meals. Within the chapter house, two or three tiers of seating, where the monks would sit during meetings, were carved into the stone. The chapter house would also prove to be of particular importance to the Knights Templar, as we shall see in a further chapter.

As we stood in the chapter house at Rievaulx Abbey, Stephen, himself a Freemason, could not help but draw a comparison between the layout of the Cistercian chapter house and that of so many typical masonic lodge rooms that he had seen. Although masonic lodges do not have a rounded apse, like the Cistercian chapter houses they do face eastward. Also, in the masonic degree of the Holy Royal Arch, the arch lies to the east, forming a rounded east end, at least after a fashion. It is also interesting to reflect that Royal Arch Freemasons meet not in lodges but in "chapters".

Second largest of the abbey's structures was the refectory or dining hall. It was so large, in fact, that many visitors to the average ruined Cistercian abbey may at first mistake it for the church itself. It was here that the monks ate their one daily meal consisting of bread and vegetables, with leeks and beans being the staple. We will look more closely at the dietary standards of the monks in the next chapter concerning their daily life. Built into the west wall of the refectory was a pulpit where daily bible readings would take place during the meal. The Cistercian brothers were almost uniquely in the course of their day allowed to speak during the meal, though only when there was something important and relevant to say.

So far we have looked at the church, cloister, chapter house and refectory. All of these aspects of the abbey are found in other monastic institutions, be they Cluniac, Benedictine or Augustinian. The initial major difference between Cistercian houses and those of other orders lies in the lack of ornamentation, which the Cistercians wholeheartedly believed was a distraction from their worship of God. The Cistercian abbey contained the simplest of vestments. The altar was not adorned with silk and lace, but rather was covered with a simple plain white cloth. Light shone not through coloured stained-glass, but through a simple unadorned window, with virtually the only light available being the natural light pouring in through the

windows of the church. There was no golden crucifix but rather
one or sometimes two iron candlesticks and a plain wooden
cross upon the Cistercian altar. The priest wore no fine silken
vestments, but a plain garment of non-dyed wool, made by the
brother monks from the fleece of the many sheep in the
monastery's care. In the main, the very modern, present-day
church at Citeaux still reflects the same sense of austerity
evident in the earliest Cistercian churches.

Another major difference between Benedictine and Cistercian
sites, aside from the lack of ornamentation, is the lengths to which
the Cistercians went to in order to provide an ample and constant
water supply. Of course all monastic communities required
water, but the Cistercians shunned wells and always sought fresh,
running water before they even considered exploiting a particular
site. One of the reasons for selecting land on or near a river was
that the Cistercians were particularly efficient with regard to
water usage. Water would be dammed and routed so as to provide
a freshwater supply to the kitchens, wash areas and reredorters
(toilets). Cistercian plumbing is incredible and we spent a great
deal of our time whilst visiting the Cistercian abbeys awestruck
by the genius behind the methods employed to provide for a safe
and sanitary environment. To modern eyes, this matter seems a
case of necessity, but we must remember that this all occurred at
a time when even royalty rarely enjoyed such luxuries as a
constantly piped supply of drinking and washing water.

Cistercian toilets were well ahead of the highest luxury
experienced by the nobility of the time. Called reredorters, they
were built elevated over a fast part of the river or stream,
carefully channelled for the specific purpose. These were
always placed on the downward side of the building, from
where the wastes would be carried downstream and away from
the abbey.

The Cistercians were adept at building irrigation channels
and dams. Water would be channelled to flow through the
kitchen, providing a fresh supply for cooking, then on to the
wash-basin set into the wall of the cloister, where the monks

would do their laundry and wash their hands and heads before entering the refectory for the daily meal. Water passed through pewter and lead, mined and smelted by the Cistercians themselves, to the refectory where it would lie in troughs for the washing of feet. This was a custom that was performed weekly as part of the religious ceremony.

There can be no question that cleanliness was an important part of Cistercian life and we can find in this aspect a parallel with the much earlier monastic order, the Essenes of Qumran and other locations in the Jordan Valley.

Another major departure in the case of Cistercian monasteries, when viewed alongside the houses of other orders, was their habit of incorporating work and prayer in an architectural as well as a philosophical sense. In most Benedictine foundations, it would have been deemed odd to have anything more industrious than a scriptorium within the precincts of the abbey itself. A cursory glance at any Cistercian house will show that the exact reverse was true in their building complexes. Fountains Abbey, for example, once had an extremely large wool-sorting house which was positioned close to the chapter house at the very heart of the central range of buildings. At Rievaulx, we walked around the extensive tannery that was positioned immediately below and alongside the refectory. It was plain from the scale of the undertaking that in its time this aspect of Rievaulx represented something much more than a way of supplying the leather and vellum necessary for this one abbey. A degree of specialization tended to develop in many Cistercian houses, commensurate with the potential of the site. In addition to acting as a self-sufficient unit, each house was therefore part of the larger Cistercian family and provided material needs from within the order as a whole. This specialization could go to almost any lengths. As an example, Melrose in Scotland showed a wonderful propensity for the construction of farm carts which served many other abbeys and were also sold into the community as a whole.

Having looked at the physical reality of the Cistercian abbey, it now remains to concentrate on the monks themselves. How did they live and what tasks and duties filled the average day of the twelfth-century Cistercian brother? We were intrigued by the rigours and hardship of the monastic, wilderness existence as much as we were by Cistercian ingenuity. And in a world of historical research that has always concentrated on the Templars as a unique and distinct order, we were already becoming very aware that this was not the case at all. The daily duties, order of service, manual labour and lifestyle of the early Cistercian monk were to give us a much better understanding of what lay behind the Templar continuum.

Chapter 10

The Cistercian's Day

The Cistercian day was delicately balanced between the two aspects of life, work and prayer, and neither was more or less important than the other. The same would be true of the Templars, though of course the nature of their labours would be rather different. Manual toil was itself considered the highest form of prayer. Both Cistercian and Templar daily life conformed to a rigid timetable which proved to be the springboard to the success of the orders.

In early medieval Europe there were no accurate clocks. For this reason, the whole of Christendom slept and rose in accordance with the natural cycles of dusk and dawn. The business of the abbey conformed to these patterns too, though the Cistercians also kept a night vigil.

The Cistercian day began at about 1.30 in the morning, when monks would rise from the simple straw mats that lay on the floor of their dormitories and make their way in silence to the night stairs leading directly from their dormitories to the church. Here in the choir stalls, the monks would take at least an hour or more to celebrate matins and lauds. The overall length of devotions was entirely dependant upon the time of year, with longer religious celebrations in winter.

The monks would assemble in the chapter house at about 4.30 a.m. Chapter meetings were important to the order and harsh consequences followed lateness or absence. Chapter was the focus of a monk's life because, in addition to the reading of a chapter from the rule of St Benedict, many other important matters were discussed. In chapter, the brethren would confess their sins and the sins of other brothers to which they were privy. It was believed that this form of "mutual justice" led to the very heart of a spiritual life. There are reflections here with modern Templarism and Freemasonry, as well as many other fraternal orders. We have come to believe that some credit for the structure of such institutions probably belongs in the abbeys of the Cistercian monks, as well as in the presbyteries of the Templars.

Democratic-style discussions on matters affecting the monastery would take place in chapter – a far cry from the excesses of feudal repression that strangled individual opinions beyond the abbey gates. Democratic-style self-government, albeit led by strong abbots, was one of the keys to the early success of the order. It was not uncommon for a young monk to quickly rise on his merits to a lofty status ahead of a more seasoned member of the order. What really mattered were commitment and zeal. Such was the case with St Bernard, who was made abbot of Clairvaux after only three years though, of course, family influence may have played a part in this rapid rise to power.

At the close of chapter, the monks would return to their quarters to collect the tools of their trade and then move on to their prescribed daily tasks. Whether working in the field, the smelting process, tannery or scriptorium, the monks made haste to get to their appointed stations, for this was as important in terms of devotion as any of the offices of the Church.

At different abbeys, and at varying periods, Cistercian monks were involved in mining, sheep-rearing, smelting and the manufacture of vellum (from calf and sheepskins) used in bookmaking. So extensive were Cistercian activities that they could not all be contained on the abbey grounds. For this reason, the Cistercians maintained "granges" or remote farms, many of which were a good day's walk from the abbey itself – some further still. This posed a great problem for the order as no choir monk could be away from the abbey at night, and certainly could not miss a service or chapter meeting. The lay brotherhood was created, in part, to fill this need.

Lay brethren, or "*conversus*" as they were called, were Cistercian monks introduced by Stephen Harding when he created the first Cistercian grange at Clos Vougeot during his abbacy at Citeaux in France. These lay brethren were of less noble stock than the choir monks and more often than not were peasants. They were certainly unlettered men and it was required that they remain so. They were monks, but the nature of their vows allowed them to work on the granges and in the mining operations without breaking the rules of the order. Once again, there are strong parallels with the Templar order in which, as we shall presently see, the Templar "knights" effectively represented the "fighting choir monk", with attendant lay staff to service their needs.

In any given abbey, lay monks far outnumbered the choir monks. Once again, this is a trend that continued in the order of the Temple, where complementary Templar staff outweighed the number of knights by a margin of ten to one. The rank of lay monk was immediately popular. Being accepted in this role offered the medieval European peasant an opportunity unparalleled in the Christian world of the day: a roof over one's head, a meal in one's belly and a spiritual purpose in one's life. The additional requirements of the religious life were not exhaustive and at least offered the chance of eternal redemption. The influx of free labour offered by the lay brethren was a masterstroke and would propel the order into economic ventures, the likes of which had not been seen previously. That these are reflected by the slightly later Templars is not surprising, bearing in mind the common roots. Templars were essentially Cistercians on horseback.

The grange system of farming, introduced by Stephen Harding

in the early part of the twelfth century, would prove to be not only successful, but also flexible. In France and Switzerland, winemaking and the growing of other crops proved economically viable, while in England sheep-rearing dominated Cistercian grange activities. So important was sheep-rearing that the Cistercians virtually cornered the European wool market. Available figures show that Fountains Abbey alone possessed at least 128,000 head of sheep, with Rievaulx and Jervaulx at 14,000 and 12,000 respectively. From just these three abbeys, they could generate an annual export of nearly 200 sacks of wool.

Known for not only the quantity, but also the quality of their wool, the Cistercians were sought out by Italian and Flemish fabric-makers to engage in long-term and binding contracts. Merchants preferred dealing with the Cistercians because they were offered continuity of production. In addition, they need only deal with the abbey "cellarer", the man charged with looking after the foundation's material and financial responsibilities. It was, for the merchants, a "one stop" operation, infinitely preferable to dealing with masses of small operators. The Templars also became great rearers of sheep and almost certainly contributed to better sheep breeds by bringing new stock from the Middle East.

The Cistercians lived free from all forms of tax, though they did occasionally fall foul of an avaricious monarch or political necessity. For example, in 1193 the Cistercians handed over an entire year's supply of wool in order to help ransom England's Richard I from captivity in Germany.

The rearing of sheep and cattle led to the production of vellum. Vellum is fine tanned leather used in the production of monastic books. Each tannery, such as the one still to be seen at Rievaulx, represented a vast array of low vats. Being located on the abbey grounds, working in the tannery would have been one of the activities that fell to the responsibility of the choir monks who, in all likelihood, never saw the animal from which the hide was taken or even the brother monk who raised it to adulthood.

Work in the tannery and other abbey-related tasks would

continue throughout the morning until the hour of 11.00 a.m. when a bell would toll, calling the monks to the service of sext. This ceremony brought the morning's activities to a close and was the precursor to a much deserved lunch. By this time, the monks had already been awake for nearly twelve hours.

Before entering the refectory or dining hall, the monks would wash their heads and hands in the wash-basin built into the cloister wall. This was important, both religiously and practically, as certainly much filth had accumulated on their hands during the morning's labours. This was the only time during the monastic day that washing occurred. In fact, bathing was generally frowned on, which is odd since the monks took such pains in the cleanliness of their surroundings and the abundance of fresh water for cleaning purposes. The ritual of "*mandatum*" or the washing of feet was regularly performed on Saturdays during certain parts of the year and served a practical as well as an ecclesiastical purpose. The apparent lack of personal hygiene amongst the monks merely represents medieval views of cleanliness, together with an ever-zealous desire to "leave one's body" at the abbey gate.

This meal consisted of vegetables, bread and leeks, for the monks were essentially vegetarian, save for special holy days when eggs and/or fish would be served. Meat was not totally absent from the monastery as those brethren who had fallen ill and who were in the infirmary were fed meat to aid their recovery – probably poultry or mutton. Meals were originally eaten in silence. Biblical passages were read and the meal ended with a "grace" and then a short service in the church.

Afternoon brought the brethren back to their labour until the hour of 6.00 p.m. when vespers would be performed. This was followed by the evening meal which consisted of the obligatory vegetables, fruit and whatever bread remained from the noon meal. Following this light meal, the monks would meet in the cloister to hear a reading of the "collation" by one of the brethren. The reading was, in turn, followed by the final service of the day which was held generally around 7.30 p.m. This service was very short by comparison to many the Cistercians practised, and generally the monks would retire by 8.00 p.m. to get their daily five hours sleep before arising to start the daily round again.

Cistercian monks toiled for an average of 133 hours per week, which is about a month's worth of work by modern standards. Such dedication was certain to lead to the success of the order. It is remarkable to observe the legacy modern society and the advance of the Industrial Age owes to the aching backs of Cistercian monks.

Chapter 11

The Templars

It is doubtful that the reader will have come this far in our journey without being acutely aware of the meteoric rise and fall of the order of the Knights Templar. As we have indicated, orthodox historical sources tell us that the Templars began as a group of nine knights under the tutelage of the first grand master Hugh de Payens. Hugh had the ear and the support of the king of Jerusalem, Baudoin II. Our own research had shown that Baldwin was a kinsman of Godfroi de Boullion. Godfroi we knew had been born of Salt Line nobility and captured Jerusalem for the Troyes Fraternity in 1099. The original nine Templar knights were granted the area under the southeast corner of the Temple Mount called Solomon's Stables (although the stables are more likely to date from the Herodian era). In addition, Baudoin granted the knights the al-Aqsa Mosque, which is on the Mount proper in the southern end above the Stables. This area of the Mount would be the Templars' principal residence for over seventy years, until the fall of Jerusalem after the Battle of Hattin in 1187.

The initial band of knights took three vows, generally believed to be those of poverty, chastity and obedience. However, the matter of a vow of poverty may be somewhat misleading. The actual translation of that part of the Templar rule is: "the keeping of goods in common". This is a far cry from an outright declaration of poverty. The intention seems to have been that no one Templar knight might own anything personally, but rather, that everything material acquired by the Templars belonged to the order. This would allow the order to grow very wealthy, as in fact it did, without breaking the original established rules. The eventual wealth, as we showed in our previous book *The Warriors and the Bankers*, came through a variety of business opportunities including banking and other mercantile ventures.

The Templars rose in a short span of time from a group of nine comrades to an army of thousands of well-trained knights. Was this accomplished through self-determination, or the assistance of the king of Jerusalem? While both of these factors played a role in the order's advancement, we feel that one need look no further for the orders success and true support than to those white-mantled monks whom occupied the cloisters of Europe for the two decades before the Templars came into being.

By the time of the Council of Troyes in 1129, Bernard of Clairvaux had been in the Cistercian order for nearly two decades, having joined in 1112. In that short time, he had risen from the status of a choir monk to becoming the abbot of his own abbey, Clairvaux. A gifted speaker and thinker, he was deemed one of the principal spokesmen of all Christendom and had the ear of king and pope alike. Bernard was selected to assist in the writing of the Templar rule of order which he patterned after the rule of his own Cistercian brotherhood. So from the very beginning, the Knights Templar followed the monastic rule of the Cistercians. This rule was, as we have indicated elsewhere, a stricter version of the original rule of St Benedict.

Bernard's support for the order of the Temple would not end with his writing of the institution's rules of conduct. Sometime between the Council of Troyes and Hugh de Payens' death around 1136, Bernard wrote a document that would do as much to assist the Templar order as the Papal Bull that granted them a tax-free status. This document was called *De Laude Novae Militae*. We know it by the English name, *In Praise of the New Knighthood*. The document is in reality a letter to Hugh de Payens, who on several occasions asked Bernard to write specifically in support of the new order. In the preamble to the chapters we find the following:

> If I am not mistaken my dear Hugh, you have asked me not once or twice, but three times to write a few words of exhortation for you and your comrades. You say that if I am not permitted to wield the lance, at least I might direct my pen against the tyrannical foe, and that this moral, rather than material support of mine will be of no small help to you. I have put you off now for quite some time, not that I disdain your request, but rather lest I be blamed for taking it lightly and hastily. I feared I might botch a task which could be better done by a more qualified hand, and which would perhaps remain, because of me, just as necessary and all the more difficult.
>
> Having waited thus for quite some time to no purpose, I have now done what I could, lest my inability should be mistaken for unwillingness. It is for the reader to judge the result. If some perhaps find my work unsatisfactory or short of the mark, I shall be nonetheless content, since I have not failed to give you my best.

Some historians, among them Desmond Seward in his book *The Monks of War*, have felt that the introduction to the letter is an indication that the Templars were initially in danger of failing as an order due to a lack of members. We are inclined to disagree with this suggestion. Rather, we would see Bernard's letters to Hugh as yet another example of the work of a carefully co-ordinated ruling elite which governed both the Cistercians and the

Templars. We have chosen to call this ruling faction the "Troyes Fraternity". Bernard's letter to Hugh de Payens was a carefully composed political device and one which achieved its objectives in an almost miraculous manner. In the document as a whole, Bernard chastised the secular knighthood of the day. In at least one section, he virtually accused them of being effeminate:

> You cover your horses with silk, and plume your armour with I know not what sort of rags; you paint your shields and your saddles; you adorn your bits and spurs with gold and silver and precious stones, and then in all this glory you rush to your ruin with fearful wrath and fearless folly. Are these the trappings of a warrior or are they not rather the trinkets of a woman?

History would prove that the decorative adornments of the average knight were in stark contrast to the Templar rule. Templar knights were allowed no ornamentation whatsoever on their bridles, swords or shields. Of course, this closely mirrored the attitude of the Cistercians themselves who also avoided any form of material excess, even in their abbey churches.

Bernard's document, *De Laude Novae Militae*, swept through Christendom like a tornado and in no time the number of Templar recruits increased. At the same time donations, gifts and bequests from monarchs and barons throughout Europe were also arriving regularly on the Templar doorstep. With a staggering rapidity, the fledgling little band of nine knights grew into what we refer to as Templar Inc. Only one monastic institution, before or since, has ever expanded with the speed of the order of the Temple. The reader my not be unduly surprised to learn that this single exception is that of the Cistercians themselves.

It intrigues us to reflect that so many thousands of pages of carefully written material concerning the Templars have dealt with the order's apparent links to other religious institutions of one sort or another. For example, some writers have claimed that the order was closely allied to the Cathars of southern

France, while others have made claims that the Templars were "closet Sufis", a form of mystical Islam with which the Templar order certainly did have contact. In fact, to discover the major influence brought to bear on the Templars, and one which remained in place for the whole of Templar history, we need look no further than medieval Champagne. It was behind the walls of Clairvaux abbey that the order of the Templars had been penned, and it was the same scriptorium from which Bernard's *In Praise of the New Knighthood* appeared. Every scrap of our research shows conclusively that the Templars were "Cistercians on horseback", and it is our contention that they served the same political and religious intentions as their brother order of white monks.

The similarity between Templars and Cistercians extended to almost every facet of the daily round, and to demonstrate this fact, we will now turn our attentions to a day in the life of a Templar knight.

Chapter 12

A Day in the Life

The Templars have often been referred to as warrior monks. The terms "warrior" and "monk" would seem to most observers these days to be mutually exclusive. However, in the case of the Templars the combination does appear to have worked. The Templar brothers considered themselves bound to a spiritual quest, but they were also highly trained medieval knights, ready for battle at a moment's notice. Bernard of Clairvaux had this to say in his *De Laude Novae Militae*:

> Thus in a wondrous and unique manner they appear gentler than lambs, yet fiercer than lions. I do not know if it would be more appropriate to refer to them as monks or as soldiers, unless perhaps it would be better to recognize them as being both. Indeed they lack neither monastic meekness nor military might.

This unique blending of qualities would be the main fact that separated the order of the Temple from their Cistercian brothers. In every other respect, the similarities between the two orders are many and obvious, and it is our intention to demonstrate this fact below. Both the Cistercian and Templar rule was, at base, a modification of the rule of the Benedictines from which the Cistercian order had departed in the late eleventh century.

It is general these days to consider the Templars as warriors first and monks second. Actually, *they* would probably have seen the situation the other way round. It is certainly true that St Bernard saw the Knights Templar as his own Cistercian army; however, it was an army that commanded adherence to a strict monastic rule. Rigorously enforced, like the Cistercian model, the Templar rule laid down some very specific governances regarding daily life.

The monastic Templar's day began at 4.00 a.m., when he would rise for a religious observance known as matins, during which the Templar brother would be required to recite thirteen paternosters. It is significant that the number thirteen is frequently found in Templar ritual. Arguably, this could represent Jesus and his twelve disciples, though there may be an astrological explanation and it is a matter to which we will return presently.

Matins would be followed by the service known as prime at 6.00 a.m. and the hearing of mass. If all the orders of business had been taken care of, the Templars would be permitted a brief nap between matins and prime, but this certainly would not have always been the case. Prime would be followed by sext at around 11.30.

By the time the Templars were ready for their first meal of the day, they would have recited a total of sixty paternosters, thirty of which were spoken for the living and another thirty for the deceased. It was believed that the latter would ask God to deliver the dead from Purgatory and transport them to Paradise. The thirty paternosters for the living represented a plea that God might forgive the sins and transgressions of the living and that they may lead a better life. For many people these days, the thought of a single payer each day seems excessive, yet the Templars were so spiritually dedicated that they would recite five dozen prayers before eating their first meal. It is a testament to the religious dedication that was maintained within the order.

The first meal of the day was generally served in two sittings. The first sitting was for the full knight brothers and the second for the sergeants. While it is difficult through modern eyes to envision such a distinction of class existing within the order, we must remember that the nobility at the time were considered to be of higher status than the working classes. Like their Cistercian counterparts, the Templar knights ate their meal in absolute silence. The only speaking came from the priest, who blessed the meal, and from the clerk who would give the Bible reading during the meal. While conducting field research for this book, we have had occasion to visit abbeys in England, Scotland and France. We never ceased to speculate as to the sound of these constant scripture readings echoing out through the cold stone walls of the refectory, met by the utter silence of hundreds of Cistercians or Templars eating their food.

Whilst the circumstances of meals were similar in the Cistercian and Templar orders, there was one major difference. The original Cistercians enjoyed an entirely vegetarian diet, with plenty of beans to make up for the protein loss. The Templars meanwhile were allowed to eat meat. In fact, it was mandatory for Templar brothers to consume meat on at least three days of the week. The thinking behind this practice was quite simple. It was believed that, as warriors, the Templars needed the strength that only a meat-rich diet could offer. The authors of the Templar rule were well aware of the corrupting influence of meat on the human body, but equally aware of the necessity of eating it, as clause 26 of the original rule clearly indicates:

It should be sufficient for you to eat meat three times a week, except at Christmas and All Saints for it is understood that the custom of eating flesh corrupts the body. But if a fast when meat must be forgone falls on a Tuesday, the next day let it be given to the brothers in plenty. And on Sundays all the brothers of the Temple, the chaplains and the clerks shall be given two meat meals in honour of the holy resurrection of Jesus Christ. And the rest of the household, that is to say the squires and sergeants, shall be content with one meal and shall be thankful to God for it.

The diet of meat consisted of mutton, veal, goat and fish, while the rest of the week the brethren would be served meals more in keeping with that of their Cistercian counterparts. These simpler meals comprised vegetable dishes and bread. They would be served two or sometimes three times a day.

Following the afternoon meal, the brethren would gather in the chapel to give thanks for the meal they had just finished. Next came nones at 2.30 p.m. and vespers at 6.00 p.m. Having arisen at 4.00 a.m., the bulk of the Templar's day, with the exception of the afternoon meal, had been engaged in prayer and devotions of one form or another. Vespers was followed by the evening meal, which was also eaten in silence.

Compline was the last order of the day and the brethren would gather for some communal drinking, whether it was water or diluted wine. The Templars were, at the leave of the master of the house, allowed to partake of wine, but it was solely at his discretion.

Silence was an absolute must in the order and was required from the leaving of compline, through the night until matins were called the following morning. Once again, we find reference to the importance of this in the Templar rule of order. In clause 31, we find the following commentary on silence:

When the brothers come out of compline they have no permission to speak openly except in an emergency. But let each go to his bed quietly and in silence, and if he needs to speak to his squire, he should say what he has to say softly and quietly. But if by chance, as they come out of compline, the knighthood or the house has a serious problem, which must be solved before morning, we intend that the Master or a party of elder brothers, who govern the Order under the

Master, may speak appropriately. And for this reason we command that it should be done in such a manner.

A closer examination of the Templar rule would indicate to us that there was perhaps a little more to this traditional role of monastic silence than would first meet the eye. For in the next clause we find the following:

> For it is written: *In multiloquio non effugies peccatum.* That is to say that to talk too much is not without sin. And elsewhere: *Mors et vita in manibus lingue.* That is to say: Life and death are in the power of the tongue. And during that conversation we altogether prohibit idle words and wicked bursts of laughter. And if anything is said during that conversation that should not be said, when you go to bed we command you to say the paternoster prayer in all humility and pure devotion.

While the first Latin quote seems to be entirely in keeping with the concept of monastic devotion, the second quote, "Life and death are in the power of the tongue", seems a great deal harsher than ecclesiastical norms would dictate. We see this as being a reference to the importance of silence and secrecy, much like the Mafia concept of *"Omerta"*. Certainly there would be danger of knights letting slip the inner working of the order to squires who were listening a little too attentively.

And so the monastic days went on. Cistercians and Templars alike would have found little difference if they were to exchange the locations of their lives. Despite these clear and obvious parallels, we remain amazed that so few writers have even mentioned the Cistercians in connection to the order of the Temple. But, of course, the Templars existed for a particular reason, and no matter what the underlying theological considerations, they were not exclusively engaged in matters of a spiritual nature.

If the Cistercians lived by the maxim *"Ora et Labora"* or "Pray and Work", the Knights Templar lived by a similar view in that "idle hands are the tool of the Devil". For when the Templars were not at war or prayer, they were at labour. Even if tasks were simple, or perhaps demeaning, such as mending armour or fixing a horse's bridle, they were dutifully and gladly performed. The Templars, like their white monk contemporaries, each had tasks to perform, whether it was tending the pigs, goats and chickens owned by the order, or working in the fields.

The care of horses was of great concern to the knights and a matter to be dealt with after matins and compline on a daily basis. While the traditional seal of the order may well depict two knights mounted on one horse, a reference to their impoverished beginnings, this image is quite misleading. The very rule of the order permitted a knight to have as many as three horses, while the master of the order was permitted to have four. One horse was not to be favoured over another, which meant that great care must have been taken that all horses were battle ready at a moment's notice. So important were the horses to the order that one of the few exceptions for a brother leaving the meal table was if the horses were disturbed in some manner. Not only did the horse play an important role in the Templar rule, it could also lead to some harsh penalties should a brother, through neglect, lose or mistreat any of his mounts.

In any monastic order there must be strict rules and regulations. The Templar order was no exception. Upon a violation of the Templar rule, the commander would call the brethren to hear the charges against an offender. The accused brother would confess of his fault and was asked to leave the room. At this time, the commander would seek the advice of the brethren in what penance to apply. If his infraction was small, or if he was found to be innocent, then no penance would be given. If, however, he was in violation of a major infraction of the rule, he would later be tried by the general chapter. We see in this self-government a form of democratic behaviour completely in keeping with the ideals of the Cistercians and the Troyes Fraternity. This trend was in stark contrast to the form of Carolingian feudalism that so dominated the world outside the Templar forts and Cistercian abbeys.

There were two basic forms of punishment within the order. The first was referred to as "losing one's coat". Losing the coat of the order was a penance of shame. Stripped from a guilty brother were his coat, weapons and horse. He would also be forced to eat from the floor, do menial tasks and be generally separated from his brethren. Such penalties were imposed for infractions such as losing a horse through neglect, loaning Templar assets without the permission of the order or threatening to join the Saracens. Having sexual relations with a woman would also result in the losing of one's coat, but was not considered as serious as homosexuality, which resulted in expulsion from the order, the harshest of all penalties.

Homosexuality represented a major accusation during the Templar trials, but throughout the whole of Templar history, strict penalties resulted from its practice and great pains were taken to prevent it. For example the Templars were commanded to sleep with candles burning. This was believed to stave off the natural lust that the darkness would generate. However, there were many other infractions of the rule that would result in expulsion from the order. The following represents a few examples:

Murdering a Christian.

Divulging the Chapters meetings.

Committing acts of sodomy.

Committing an act of heresy or denouncing the Christian faith.

Conspiring or making false charges against a brother.

Leaving the Temple house for more than two days without permission.

Fleeing the enemy during battle while the Beauseant was flying or without permission of the Marshall.

Such penalties, rules and regulations were not exclusive to the Templar and Cistercian orders. Indeed, the Teutonic knights and Hospitaller orders shared rules and penalties of their own. Again, there is one striking aspect of the Templar penal system that solidifies the similarities between the two orders. A Templar knight, upon being found guilty of an infraction punishable by expulsion from the order, was not simply turned out into the street. By the very rule he had been read at his initiation, the expelled Templar was obligated to join another monastic order in the hope of saving his soul. It is very telling that the only religious order available to an erring and expelled Templar knight was that of the Cistercians. It is perhaps this fact, more than any other, which highlights the similarities and interdependence of the two institutions.

Chapter 13

A Daring Plan

Everything that we had learned so far about the Cistercians, and the group of Burgundian and Flemish families who had inspired the foundation of this most remarkable monastic institution, led us to believe that orthodox history had missed something very important in its handling of the white monks and in its understanding of the motives that lay behind the founding of the order.

Few accounts written so far have specifically made mention of the deep Burgundian connections at the heart of Cisterciansim. What we suggest is that the formation of the Cistercians, and later the Templars, represents part of a cohesive plan, the ultimate intention of which was to change the political and religious complexion of Europe. The fact that this endeavour is not reported in letters 10 metres high across the annals of history is not surprising. It was never intended to be known or understood by anyone, with the exception of specific representatives of the families in question. We would argue that by the year 1307, when the French crown made its now famous attack on the Templar movement, some, if not all, of the Burgundian plan was beginning to become obvious outside the closed circle of initiates that stood at its heart. However, with a few notable exceptions, medieval monarchs, and even popes of the eleventh and twelfth centuries, were far from being gifted with great foresight or even startling intelligence, and so it may not have been too difficult for the agencies in question to keep the kings of the Franks in the dark for many decades.

Members of this select band of mainly Salt Line families seem to have chosen the Champagne city of Troyes for their headquarters throughout most of the period in question, and it therefore seems entirely appropriate to refer to those putting the various parts of the plan into action as the Troyes Fraternity. The reader will recall that, historically, Champagne had not existed at the time of the First Crusade and that Troyes, previous to this period, was merely a large city within the confines of Burgundy. Many of the aristocratic families of Troyes still had Burgundian holdings and were blood-tied to the rulers of Burgundy. By the start of the twelfth century, Troyes was already acquiring the reputation of being one of the most important cultural capitals of Europe. The city was also centrally placed between Burgundy to the south and Flanders to the north. As a meeting place for the shadowy planners of this ambitious scheme, it was second to none.

Further north than Troyes, the Mayors of the Palace, that family group that had successfully usurped the Frankish thrones of France at the time of the death of Dagobert II in the seventh century, spared little time in seeking to establish a very different sort of Europe for themselves and their descendants. A succession of Carolingian monarchs, as the dynasty came to be known, successfully engineered changes in both social structure and the working practices of the Catholic Church. So powerful did these rulers become that opponents to their rule, from within the territories they controlled, would have risked ultimate ruin had they chosen to stand openly against developing feudalism or what would eventually come to be known as Roman Catholicism.

The Carolingians has set upon a deliberate policy of destroying forever the old Roman style of government, together with earlier Christian religious practices. Anyone from the minor, middle or even higher aristocracy who made the slightest move against the Carolingians was dealt with summarily, and with all the barbarity that would become the hallmark of feudal, dictatorial monarchs.

Burgundy, meanwhile, had a long and illustrious past of its own and was often a thorn in the side of the Carolingians. One of the last truly independent kings of the larger Burgundy was called Gundobad, and he reigned from 474 until 516. He was of Germanic stock and was one of a strong breed of local leader who kept some sort of stability going in the region after the withdrawal of the Romans.

King Gundobad was a contemporary of the Merovingian King Clovis. The wife of Clovis, Clotilde, the woman who is supposed to have persuaded Clovis to be baptized, was Gundobad's niece. Gundobad was a Christian himself, probably of the Arian persuasion, but it is known that in later life he sided with the Roman Church. Once again, it is important to point out that this was the pre-feudal Catholic Church and not the Roman Catholic institution that would be introduced at a later date.

King Gundobad was a very forward-looking monarch by the standards of the day, and introduced two specific laws, both geared towards establishing a broad and fair legal system within his domains. These two laws were called, respectively, the *Lex Gundobada* and the *Lex Romana Burgundionum*. Not long after the death of Gundobad, Burgundy fell to Merovingian domination and for a short while it became part of the larger Merovingian kingdom.

With the death in 679 of Dagobert II, whom we have seen is often considered to be the last of the Merovingians, power further north came into the hand of the Mayors of the Palace, who instituted the Carolingian dynasty. The same was not true of Burgundy, however. As early as 561, when the Merovingian King Clotaire had died, Burgundy had become a separate Merovingian kingdom under rule one of Clotaire's sons, Guntrum.

Burgundy remained in the hands of the Merovingian monarchs until the early eighth century when it was annexed by Charles Martel, grandfather of the more famous Charlemagne. Burgundy was at this stage effectively under the rule of the Carolingians. However, things soon changed again because in 877 along came the charmingly named Boso to take it from them. Boso was not of Carolingian blood, and was the son of Buvin, Count of the Ardennes, another region that only nominally owed allegiance to the Carolingian crown. The reign of Boso was probably pivotal to the later history of Burgundy and to the evolution of the Troyes Fraternity.

Boso was the brother-in-law of Charles the Bald, King of the West Franks. Charles gave Boso control over Lombardy. With the advent of the minority of the Frankish monarchs Louis III and Carloman, Boso took the opportunity to insist that the bishops of Provence crown him as king of Burgundy. He temporarily expanded the region under his control, and repeatedly fought against Carolingian incursions.

The region called Burgundy altered in geographical shape and changed hands several times during the next century, and its fate was only finally settled a few decades before the First Crusade. From 1032 Burgundy was in the hands of the Capetian family, a branch of which was destined, through Hugh Capet, to overthrow the Carolingian dynasty and take the throne of the Franks in 987. Hugh Capet was descended from the Dukes of Blois and, though related to the rulers of Burgundy, he did not control their territory. In fact, he only really held a small amount of land around Paris and it was only later in the dynasty of the Capetians that the various elements of what had been the Merovingian kingdom were once again stitched together to approximate something like the France of today. In time, Burgundy would toe the Capetian line and broadly follow the dictates of the early kings of France, but the situation at the end of the eleventh century was not at all clear-cut and Burgundy represented an autonomous and independent state. The city of Troyes did not fall into the hands of the Paris-based Capetians until 936, and it responded heavily to Burgundian influence for a long period after this time. Our research indicates that during the whole period between the death of Dagobert II in 679 and the beginning of the fourteenth century, when it fell to the French crown, Troyes steered a Burgundian path and adhered strongly to the ideals and values that had predominated during the reign of the Merovingians.

It is interesting to set these historical findings against the research of Baigent, Leigh and Lincoln in their book *The Holy Blood and the Holy Grail*. The general thrust of the argument in this book is that there existed, for many centuries, a strongly allied group of families, the sole intention of which was to reinstate a Merovingian king on the throne of France. As we have previously mentioned, it is suggested that this dynasty carried in its veins the blood of Jesus and therefore the Royal House of David. Whilst we can personally find no conclusive evidence to substantiate what must be considered a very contentious assertion, neither can we deny that support for a Merovingian-style monarchy appears to have perpetuated in the region long after the dynasty was extinguished. It would have been quite natural for the ruling families of Burgundy to be allied to such a notion.

Although we might find ourselves taking task with Baigent, Leigh and Lincoln's supposition that the support for the Merovingian monarchs extended down to almost the present day, the general theme set out in *The Holy Blood and the Holy Grail* is at least probably true up to and beyond the time of the First Crusade. At this stage of history, descendants of the Merovingian dynasty did still exist, quite apart from the supposition that the son of Dagobert II had survived and provided further male heirs. However, it is very probable that it was not the Merovingians specifically that were of interest to the Troyes Fraternity, but more the sort of government and religious observance they had perpetuated.

The ancestors of the Merovingians had moved westward into northern Gaul when the Roman legions were forced to withdraw. Although the Franks as a whole would come to fight tenaciously against each other, their entry into the region we now call France was more or less unopposed. They were hard but fair rulers and had for many centuries been under the wing of the Roman imperial machine, which they generally understood and perpetuated in their own form of government. There is no evidence that they attempted to eradicate indigenous populations in the areas that ultimately fell under their sway, and they provided something of a buffer against the excesses of petty feudal warlords who might have been expected to enforce their will on the population following the fragmenting of Roman rule.

As we have seen, Christianity came early to these people when Clovis was baptized sometime around 498. Despite this fact, much of his rapidly growing kingdom remained heathen. Surprisingly, the gradual conversion of those peoples who fell under the sway of the Merovingians were not achieved by monks from Rome, as might have been expected, but by itinerant Irish monks, thus ensuring a strong Culdean-type influence in Merovingian religion. British saints in general were popular in the courtly circles of Clovis and his immediate descendants. As an example, the holy relics of St Alban were housed at a monastery built by Clovis. It should also be recalled that the young Dagobert II, fleeing from the machinations of the Mayors of the Palace, found a safe haven amongst the Culdeans of Ireland and then, finally, England.

Merovingians could be seen to follow a non-heretical, Culdean religious path, but the heretical sect of Arianism was rife amongst other Frankish Christian groups, particularly the Burgundians to the south. Although this was something that the ecclesiastical authorities of the time could not tolerate, the general pattern during the reign of Clovis and his immediate descendants was towards religious freedom within orthodox Christianity. The business of the Church was conducted in the local tongue and, as with the British and Irish Churches, some liberality regarding forms of worship was tolerated amongst the

Merovingians, just as long as the basic dogmas of the faith were seen to be upheld.

Politically speaking, the Merovingians sowed the seeds of their own demise very early in their history. Following a roughly Roman practice, they enlisted support from powerful civil servants who eventually became known as Mayors of the Palace. Thanks to a series of minority kings, the Mayors gradually amassed more and more power until they were eventually able to topple the royal family altogether and replace it with their own.

With the Carolingians came a rapid change in governmental forms and (as we have seen) the start of a constant struggle between State and Church as to ecclesiastical power and self-government. A rigid autocracy made demands that some of the landed families in the region must have found difficult to swallow. Burgundy, in particular, harboured all manner of "fringe" Christians. The Burgundians had been associated with the Roman Empire for centuries and were probably the repository of extremely old forms of the religion, some of which were almost certainly of Eastern rather than strictly Roman origin. In addition, it seems that the old ceremonial 'Is' sites, where the Black Madonnas were situated, still held a particular fascination for the local populace. The simple truth seems to be that there was a cross-section of landowning families of ancient descent, who were probably not Christian at all in the Roman Catholic sense of the word. Ways in which they differed from orthodoxy would be made manifest in some of the accusations levelled at the Knights Templar in the early fourteenth century.

With the consolidation of Carolingian rule, people who for centuries had been able to practise their own forms of religious worship, provided they did not show themselves to be totally heretical, were put under pressure to toe not only a religious line that they found impossible, but also to condone the onset of feudalism, which ran absolutely counter to their imperial and tribal backgrounds.

It is almost certain that the mainly Salt Line families in question considered themselves to be the natural repository of a belief pattern and of a particular way of looking at the world that they knew to be truly ancient. From within their midst had sprung the officiating priesthood of this "old way" – those individuals who eventually coalesced into the Druids of the Celts and into the first Culdean monks, but whose lineage was infinitely older than either. They were part of an extremely archaic tradition and held positions, at least within their own lands, that they would not lightly relinquish.

These families were almost exclusively of Salt Line origin, legatees of thousands of years of unbroken tradition. Their beliefs had been modified and synthesized, but there was clearly something very special about the way they saw themselves. To reconstruct their specific religious and political beliefs would be almost impossible, though we suggest that the Cistercian and Templar ideals, both of which were absolutely divorced from the political norms of the period into which they arose, offer some clue as to the motivation of the Troyes Fraternity and their more historically distant cousins.

But even if there was a cohesive and, of necessity, fairly silent opposition to the ever-tightening grip of Carolingian authority during the eleventh century, what could an obvious minority do to alter the western European status quo? No matter how respected they might be within their own domains, these family groups did not represent the majority of the population and so armed rebellion would have been out of the question. It is probable that all manner of suggestions were made in the dark recesses of the palace of Troyes during the second half of the eleventh century. We will never know if the final decisions came from one agency or were the result of many hours of argument and counter suggestion. But when the final plans were approved, probably at the start of the last decade of the eleventh century, they proved to be little short of brilliant. We may not be able to put a name or a face to the specific strategists who set in play a series of brave, ingenious and cunning actions, but their effect blazes like a bright star against the drab skyline of feudal France.

One simple strategy stands at the heart of the whole venture, and it can be seen in operation time and again in the years between 1050 and the middle of the twelfth century. At its heart lay the knowledge that small actions, if employed carefully and at the right time, can have great consequences. The members of the Troyes Fraternity were not without influence, particularly throughout Burgundy, and nowhere is this influence more obvious than within the forces ruling the Vatican during this pivotal period.

We have already demonstrated the way St Bernard of Clairvaux was able to manipulate the popes of his period in order to gain his own objectives, but this habit was already established even before St Bernard was born. The process began with the election of Pope Urban II in 1088. Actually, it may have commenced even before this because there are indications that the strategy was of an earlier origin, possibly dating back to the installation of Pope Gregory VII in 1073, though the circumstances which the Troyes Fraternity sought to put its plans into action never materialized during Gregory's reign.

Urban II was a different matter altogether. The real name of this pontiff was Odo of Chatillon-sur-Marne, and he was born in Champagne of a family that could well have been allied to the Burgundian cause. Exactly how far Urban's personal sympathies might have extended along the road to Troyes is difficult to assess and it seems more likely that he was simply an extremely useful tool in the hands of men who were ready to set their plans into action. Certainly Urban II was approachable and was probably personally known to the ruling house of Champagne. He had trained at Cluny which, as we have seen, was a Burgundian monastery and the place that ultimately supplied the first Cistercian monks. What probably appealed most about Urban to the Troyes Fraternity was that he was a natural reformer.

He was elected pope in 1088, the legatee of a desire, leading back ultimately to Gregory VII, to clean up the Church. In particular, he was fiercely opposed to state control of the investiture of priests and bishops. He strongly disapproved of the priesthood marrying and showed a great desire to reunite the Christian Churches of West and East. All of these qualities and beliefs were undoubtedly of interest to the Troyes Fraternity, though entirely for their own reasons, but what appealed most was Urban's enthusiasm for a crusade to wrest the Holy Land from the grip of the Turks.

Whether or not this desire was instilled in Urban by the very agencies in Champagne and Burgundy that were his best supporters against the anti-Pope Clement III is uncertain, though his actions clearly played right into the hands of the Troyes Fraternity. By 1095 Urban was secure enough to call a great council at Clermont-Ferrand in central southern France. There, on the longitudinal Salt Line that passes close to the west of the city, he spoke out against lay appointments of priests and bishops, outlawed marriages for his priests and, most famously of all, called for the forces of Christianity to launch a crusade against the Turks.

The response was immediate and enthusiastic. This is not surprising for any number of reasons. The population of France had risen rapidly and there were many thousands of the sons of nobles simply itching for a holy quest that might also provide substantial wealth to their family coffers – a crusade offered the best chance of gaining both spiritual and material gains. From the perspective of the pope, the prospect of a crusade might strengthen the fragile ties between the Christians of the East and those of western Europe. It would also serve to take some of the heat out of the feudal disputes that ravaged so much of the West at this time and, hopefully, rid all regions of a number of hotheaded, would-be warlords that it could well do without. Specifically fuelled by the enthusiasm of agencies within Champagne, Burgundy and Flanders, plans for the crusade went ahead at a pace.

By 1099 the crusaders were at the gates of Jerusalem itself, and what was more important from the perspective of the Troyes Fraternity was that the leader of the forces besieging the Holy City was Godfroi de Bouillon. If Godfroi, the tall, blond but not especially clever Flemish count, was not actually an active member of the Troyes Fraternity, he was certainly one of its pawns. We have already detailed his strong Salt Line pedigree and there is evidence, discussed presently, for believing that he probably was not as feeble-minded as history has asserted, and that he may have been knowingly and deliberately working under the strict instructions of the selfsame agencies that had instigated the crusade in the first place. On 15 July the Christian forces entered Jerusalem, putting the first part of the carefully laid plans of the Troyes Fraternity in place.

Chapter 14

Consolidation

Within days of his victory in Jerusalem in 1099, Godfroi de Bouillon, Salt Line count and blood relative of many of the members of the Troyes Fraternity, was offered the crown of Jerusalem, a singular honour that he declined, allowing himself only the rank of "Protector of the Holy Sepulchre". Pope Urban did not survive long enough to see the victory; he had died earlier in the same year. Even if he had still been enthroned in the Vatican, it is hard to imagine that he could ever have realized the way he had been manipulated. His position had been used as a means to gain the first objective in an exercise that was intended to destroy the power of the Roman Church for good.

Godfroi soon followed Urban to eternal rest, probably poisoned, within a few short months of his much exalted victory. He had been a complex man. Differing historians paint him in terms that extend from well-meaning, muscle-bound village idiot on the one extreme, to elevated saint of Christendom on the other. In reality, he was probably very much a product of his background and the age into which he was born. His road to Jerusalem had been soaked in blood: Christian, Jewish and Islamic. Godfroi's ultimate success had by no means been assured, but doubtless the Troyes Fraternity had other plans up their sleeves in case he should have failed them. In the event he prevailed, and though he refused the Jerusalem crown himself, his brother Baudoin was prevailed upon to accept it.

One of the most interesting aspects of Godfroi's arrival in Jerusalem is that it is known he was attended by a virtually anonymous group of obviously very powerful individuals. Forming a sort of shadowy conclave, they appear to have wielded more power than Godfroi himself. No names have been left in antiquity to attest as to the point of origin or families of these men, but they may have included a mysterious man by the name of Peter the Hermit. Peter came from Amiens in France and, although nothing of note is known of his origins, he was one of the most influential figures of the period. Contemporary with the preaching of Pope Urban II, Peter the Hermit had also called for a crusade, though he had done more than simply preach. Ahead of the victorious armies that had travelled across Europe and then on to the Holy Land, Peter had set out with a ramshackle army of peasants. His passage to the Middle East was not a glorious one, and Peter the Hermit usually has been dismissed as a charismatic and well-meaning, but basically inept, individual. However, this version of his story may be far from the truth.

Persistent historical rumours suggest that Peter the Hermit had formerly been a tutor to Godfroi de Bouillon, and he certainly came from the right part of France to have fulfilled such a role. It is known that by 1093 he was already in Jerusalem and that after this he returned to France, to an abbey that may have been his home at some stage prior to his visit to the Middle East. This was an institution founded at Orval, close to Stenay in the Ardennes, where Dagobert II had been murdered. Mathilde de Toscane, Duchess of Lorraine and Godfroi de Bouillon's aunt, granted the land for the abbey that had been built there in 1070. Godfroi himself came to control this part of Lorraine and paid special reverence to Stenay (with its relics of the dead King Dagobert) and to Orval Abbey. Regarding the order, persuasions and even nationality of the monks there, history seems to have been wiped deliberately clean.

It appears that it was intentionally ordained by someone that all trace of this foundation should be removed from the historical record. It might have been difficult for us to establish who the individual was, were it not for the fact that the monks of Orval mysteriously left their abbey around 1108. The land, and indeed the abbey itself, ultimately came into the possession of none other than St Bernard of Clairvaux, whereupon the Cistercian abbey built there absorbed the land, and the shadowy history, of the former occupants.

One intriguing possibility, suggested by Baigent, Leigh and Lincoln, is that the monks of Orval were removed *en masse* to a new abbey that had been built for them in Jerusalem itself. Such a foundation most certainly did exist. It stood on an impressive hill outside the city walls of Jerusalem and occupied the site of a previous Byzantine church. There are plenty of records remaining that attest to the existence of this abbey, thought (but not proven) to be an Augustinian foundation. In truth it may not have been anything to do with the Augustines at all because it is best remembered as the Order of Notre Dame de Sion.

It is probably not at all presumptuous to suggest that here we find the Jerusalem headquarters of the Troyes Fraternity, which adopted the name of the Order of Sion once the Holy Land was secured. These were the selfsame individuals who tried to confer the rank of king of Jerusalem on Godfroi de Bouillon and who, when Godfroi died, would brook no refusal from his brother Baudoin. Peter the Hermit was almost certainly one of this elite group. He returned to Europe in the year 1100, very shortly after the coronation of Baudoin. Upon his return, he was immediately made prior of the abbey in Huy, Flanders, an institution which he personally founded on land granted by the family of Godfroi and Baudoin.

Another member of this "inner circle" is likely to have been Hugh, Count of Champagne. He is known to have taken part in the First Crusade, though of his movements and accomplishments, we have no record. Since he was kin to Godfroi de Bouillon, he is very likely to have been part of his entourage. The Count of Champagne was a powerful man and he would have commanded a sizeable contingent of the force that descended on Jerusalem. It is highly likely, therefore, that if we do not know anything of his exploits in Jerusalem, this is simply because he wished to remain in the background. This would be all the more understandable if he had formed part of an inner circle, the movements and strategy of which were kept quiet, especially from the Carolingian rulers and the Vatican.

It is from the Order of Notre Dame de Sion that Baigent, Leigh and Lincoln tentatively suggest that the "Prieure de Sion" ultimately derived and, furthermore, they speculate that Godfroi de Bouillon himself might have founded the order much earlier, in around 1089. If so it is hardly likely to have centred upon the same monks as those located at Orval, for Godfroi was a mere ten years of age when Orval was consecrated. However, we do have to bear in mind that the Orval monastery was made possible by an aunt of Godfroi, the woman who had been most responsible for his upbringing. It is therefore entirely possible that the family connection predated Godfroi personally. In fact, Godfroi seems to have been preparing himself for his crusading destiny for at least a decade before Pope Urban II even made his impassioned plea. We are left wondering whether Godfroi de Bouillon had about as much choice regarding the ultimate nature of his life as did St Bernard of Clairvaux.

The kingship of Jerusalem established by Godfroi and Baudoin is generally referred to by historians as being a "Frankish throne". If this statement is intended to infer some relationship with the throne of France at the time, it is certainly misleading. Godfroi and Baudoin owed their bloodlines to the Franks, but they were not of Carolingian stock. There is now little or no argument that the blood that flowed through the veins of these men was predominantly Merovingian. These first kings of Jerusalem paid no attention whatsoever to the Carolingian monarchs of northern France and were totally autonomous in their own city and its surroundings. It was with these facts in mind that the modern Prieure de Sion, that most strange institution headed by Pierre Plantard de St-Clair, claimed that Baudoin's accession to the throne of Jerusalem saw the reinstatement of the rightful Merovingian dynasty which was previously supposed to have died with Dagobert II.

It should perhaps be stated again that our research was derived from entirely different sources than those consulted by Baigent, Leigh and Lincoln in *The Holy Blood and the Holy Grail*. Nevertheless, we fully admit that there are times when we cannot fail to recognize the eerie parallels that exist between the so-called Order of Sion and the organization we chose to call the Troyes Fraternity. So many similarities exist that we are forced to conclude that they may, initially at least, have been one and the same institution.

Whether Troyes Fraternity or Order of Sion, the main thrust of the organization's activities in and around Jerusalem immediately after the fall of the city to the Christian forces is no mystery to us, since it represents one aspect of the plans so carefully hatched in Troyes and further south in Burgundy. To the Christian world as a whole, the possession of Jerusalem appeared to be a glorious thing (an attitude presumably also held at the time by the Vatican). Whether or not there were any disquieting voices echoing through Rome, even at this early date, we will never know. This would certainly have been the case if anyone occupying the Holy See had been in a position to look two decades ahead.

Baigent, Leigh and Lincoln claim to have evidence that it was this mysterious conclave, the Order of Sion, that tried to confer the title of king upon Godfroi and which later offered the crown to his brother Baudoin. If this is true, we are dealing with extremely powerful people, which is no more than might be expected if Hugh de Champagne was included in the number. Meanwhile, many hundreds of miles to the west, the second stage of the carefully laid plans was beginning to take shape.

For some time we, the authors, had both been struck by the apparent coincidence that links the fall of Jerusalem to the Christians and the foundation of the first Cistercian monastery. The first monks of Citeaux threw up their wooden buildings in 1098, by which time the crusading armies were well on their way to capturing Jerusalem, an event that actually took place in 1099. Of course there is no evidence to link the two events, but there is still much about the embryonic Cistercian order to suggest that a connection did exist. Cistercian monasticism was built on Benedictine models, but we have already seen how much it varied from these. Truly, in its reliance on a system of mother and daughter houses, it resembled the ideals of Cluny, from whence it sprang. Cluny, at its start, was also a "reformed order", and may have represented an earlier attempt by the Troyes Fraternity to create something that would ultimately have to wait for Robert of Molesmes and Stephen Harding. In almost every other regard, Cistercianism smacked at a form of monasticism that had never prevailed in the West before. True, it owed a great deal to the early Culdean houses of Britain and Ireland, but we have shown that these two may have sprung from Middle-Eastern, pre-Christian ideas.

The Cistercian order so closely resembled the way of life chosen by the Essene of the Jordan Valley that comparisons simply have to be drawn. As to how or why this might have come about, we hope to provide more evidence as our story progresses, but it relied in the most profound way possible on the belief in a "New Jerusalem".

Early Cistercian writers, such as St Stephen Harding and especially St Bernard of Clairvaux, were virtually obsessed with the concepts of Jerusalem and Sion. It should also be remembered that St Bernard was absolutely instrumental in the formation of the Knights Templar, who were specifically named after the Temple, that most revered spot of the ancient

Jews. Jerusalem was the location that also lay at the heart of Essene belief.

It is almost as if the agencies concerned in the Troyes Fraternity and the Cistercian movement were fully aware that there were direct connections between themselves and the Jews of old, which bore out our discoveries regarding a degree of Jewish involvement in the rise of the Celtic Culdean movement. It should be recalled that the original Burgundy, when at its full power, extended far down into Savoy, encompassing parts of France that had been very responsive to all manner of foreign traders back in the days of the Roman Empire. These must have included many Jews, particularly so immediately after the fall of the Jewish Levant to the forces of Rome after the Jewish uprising in AD 70.

Whether or not much earlier Jewish connections with the Troyes Fraternity can be proved, we contend that there is absolutely no coincidence between the prosecution of the First Crusade and the establishment of the first Cistercian monastery. Both courses of action were speculative and either could so easily have failed. All the same, in the comprehension of the shrewd minds at work in both enterprises, the first action – the capture of the Holy Land – could only be exploited if the correct agencies within western Europe, and especially Burgundy, were also up and running.

After the installation of Baudoin as king of Jerusalem in the year 1100, there was an eighteen-year lull in the activities of the Troyes Fraternity, or the Order of Sion as its Jerusalem outpost was most probably known. There were probably several different reasons for this state of affairs, but one remains paramount, namely the nature and difficulties of the popes who reigned during this period.

Urban II, who had been so skilfully manipulated into calling for the crusade, did not live to see Jerusalem fall to the forces of Christendom. His immediate successor was Paschal II, who reigned from 1099 until 1118. Paschal was born Ranierus and was an Italian with no connection whatsoever to the

Burgundians, the reformed Benedictines, or the newly formed Cistercians. Paschal's time as pope was disastrous for the Church. His constant struggle with the Holy Roman Emperors Henry IV and Henry V made it impossible for him to push ahead with the Church reforms that the more Burgundian-style Popes Urban II and Gregory VII had instigated. He was constantly dogged by a succession of anti-popes and showed little interest in the affairs of the far west of Europe. One can instinctively see that he would not have been a favourite with the Troyes Fraternity or the emerging Order of Sion in Jerusalem. However, it is likely that with the high degree of consolidation required in the Holy Land, and a desire to see the new Cistercian order flourishing, this halt in proceedings was not unduly problematical. It was, however, during the reign of Pope Paschal II that Bernard of Fontaine, later Bernard of Clairvaux, first entered the monastic life in 1113.

It is difficult to tell whether the next pope was any more to the liking of the Troyes Fraternity than Paschal had been. Giovanni Da Gaetan, who served as pope from January 1118 to January 1119, was known as Gelasius II. He inherited some of the problems of his predecessor, but he seemed to be more in tune with the region we would now call France, though he was an Italian by birth. Some of the arguments regarding the right of kings to appoint clergy came close to being settled during his short incumbency, though he was fairly lacking in overall success, mainly due to being in office for only a year. Gelasius did not have any personal connections with either Cluny or Citeaux, though he did die at Cluny, having come to the region to host a conference in Reims.

In his successor, the Troyes Fraternity had a definite ally because Callistus II was none other than Gui of Burgundy, son of Count William I of Burgundy. He was, therefore, in one way or another directly related to the houses of Burgundy and Champagne. Callistus II proved, during the five years of his office, to be closely allied to the Troyes Fraternity. The cardinals at Reims chose Callistus as pope upon the death of his predecessor, and one can imagine that some pressure to make this appointment may have been exerted in the heartland of Champagne. He immediately proved to be a sound reformer of the type the Troyes Fraternity obviously favoured at the time. He strongly opposed the rights of the Holy Roman Emperors and thus endeared himself to the Champagne and Burgundy factions in yet another way. It was immediately after the commencement of the reign of Callistus that the nine original Templar knights had supposedly knocked on the door of King Baudoin of Jerusalem. The acknowledgment of these knights as the founders of a genuine order had to wait for the growing influence of Bernard of Clairvaux, and the reign of a later pope.

Meanwhile Bernard was going from strength to strength. As we saw earlier, his arrival at Citeaux didn't so much represent an addition to the Cistercian order, but its virtual take-over, since he brought thirty family members with him. In 1116, he was granted land by Count Hugh de Champagne that would become the site for the Clairvaux Abbey just a few kilometres from Troyes. By this stage, the plans of the Troyes Fraternity were well on the boil.

The original Templar knights remained in Jerusalem until 1127 when most of them returned to Champagne. There, in Troyes (where else could it have been?), they were officially declared to be a monastic order sanctioned by the pope of the day, Honorius II. No pope would have been wise to refuse the request, especially since it was made by Bernard of Clairvaux, undoubtedly the most powerful man in Western Christendom by this period.

By 1127, the Cistercian order was growing at a positively meteoric rate. It already had many foundations in Burgundy and Champagne, and was about to launch a campaign to establish new ones across the Channel in Britain. Bernard was chief spokesperson for the order, but he was much more besides. Even by the comparatively tender age of thirty-seven, he was an adviser to counts, princes and kings, and would shortly be a pope maker. In fact he could quite easily have had the Holy See for himself, had be so desired the office. The fact that he never did seek the Vatican is very telling in itself.

If the success of the Cistercians was amazing, it was easily equalled by that of the Knights Templar. Perhaps part of the reason for this is that the new fighting order attracted a particular sort of person of which there were many about in France and the whole of western Europe at the time. Fighting was something that members of even the minor nobility understood, for they were raised to it from birth. Because of potential problems regarding inheritance, and often for want of something better, younger sons of noble families invariably found themselves entering the Church. As Templars, they could lead an exciting life, whilst at the same time serving a religious ideal in which they fervently believed. Templar knights had to be of good birth, but they didn't have to be rich. Crusading, except as a low-ranking foot soldier, was an expensive business. Once accepted and trained, horses, squires, armour, food and lodgings were supplied to the Templar warrior. And, though it might seem to a modern observer that the life of the Templar was pretty horrendous by the standards of today, it is surely a fact that hundreds of those who rapidly enlisted in the order must have been overjoyed at the prospect.

It was the crowning glory of the plans of the Troyes Fraternity and the Order of Sion in Jerusalem to have the Templars declared an official order, but even this was just a beginning. During the reign of Pope Innocent II, the Templars would be made responsible to no other authority than the pope himself. In other words, no civil or ecclesiastical court could touch the meanest hair on the grubbiest head of the lowliest page in the order. Undoubtedly the pope took this step for a number of reasons, some of which we have outlined in our earlier book, *The Warriors and the Bankers*:

1. Although Templar vows forbade the Templars from coming to arms with other Christians, no pope at that time could have failed to realize that to have a huge standing army of

formidable knights would obviously impress the many monarchs with whom he often found himself at odds.

2. No reasonable request made by Bernard of Clairvaux would ever have been refused by Innocent II.

3. The Templars were a monastic order, so to allow any temporal authority to have control over them would have been to retread a bitter road towards State preferment or authority over members of the Church.

4. The pope, often alienated from events in the Holy Land, would have been especially pleased to know that the largest single Christian fighting force in the area was at least nominally under his command.

Thus the primary plans of those families who had striven for so long to turn back the tide of feudalism, and whose real argument was with a Roman Catholic Church that no longer represented their religious interests, were put into place. The position of Bernard of Clairvaux was unassailable, as was that of the agency that had brought him to birth, and on whose behalf he worked so diligently.

In a very short time, Cistercian monastery begat Cistercian monastery, spreading exponentially across the face of western Europe. The strategy was brilliant and once commenced, simply because it remained so popular, it could not be stopped no matter how alarmed local rulers (and eventually popes) may have been. A similar state of affairs soon followed with the Templars. It quickly became apparent that they were far more than warriors. As we shall presently see, they were to learn quickly the lessons that had made the Cistercians into such good farmers. For every Templar knight in the field of battle, there were dozens more in the green fields of Europe. Within a decade or so, they could be found almost everywhere. Templars were to be found tending farms, shearing sheep, cutting wood, growing grain and, in fact, running their own empire in a very similar manner to their brother order, the Cistercians. Not a country was exempt and barely a county failed to be represented. The most remote highlander in Scotland or Arab shepherd boy in the Jordan Valley knew of the humility and charity of the "white monks" and the chivalry of the "white knights".

By the very nature of its calling, the Cistercian order could only grow in scale. Its monks were vowed to a peaceful life in beautiful and remote surroundings. It could become the greatest monastic order in the world, but its ability to influence the world, on its own, was always going to be limited – it needed something akin to the Templars. The Templars were, originally at least, the arms, the eyes, the legs and the swords of the Cistercians. Templars could go anywhere without fear. They represented the means by which the economic ideas of the Troyes Fraternity could be translated into practice.

Despite their monastic standing, in financial terms the Templars were honour bound to "take" and never to "give". This policy was probably adopted because to indulge in charity would have weakened the structure of the order. The Templars themselves grew great as merchants, bankers, sailors and the rest. Even if they did so for purely selfish reasons, their sheer presence in society still could not fail to make a huge difference to the local economies of a dozen countries. Our story has far to go, but even at this stage it cannot be doubted that in this respect at least, in the promulgation of an entirely new set of economic values even for their own compatriots, the plans of the Troyes Fraternity turned out to be spectacularly successful. It is just conceivable that without the spur that the Cistercians and the Templars offered to the economic life of western Europe, medieval feudalism may never have released its iron grip on the lives and souls of millions (perhaps even to this very day).

Chapter 15

The Founding Fathers

One of the greatest mysteries regarding the Templars comes at the very commencement of their existence. Considering just how famous the Templar order would become, there is surprisingly little independent evidence regarding its earliest days, at least prior to the important Council of Troyes in 1127. After this pivotal event, the light of European awareness was turned towards the order, which nevertheless maintained a degree of secrecy all the way through its existence that is quite astonishing. But prior to 1127, it seems that virtually nobody knew anything about the original Templar knights, a state of affairs which undoubtedly suited the Troyes Fraternity and the Order of Sion perfectly.

The account we have of the founding of the Templars was written some time after the events it describes. Our only informant is an historian by the name of Guillaume de Tyre. He did not pen his account until at least 1175, and probably much later, so he is writing three-quarters of a century after the events that took place in Jerusalem and immediately after its capture by the forces of Godfroi de Bouillon. As to where Guillaume came by his original material, we have hardly a clue, and it is entirely possible that his whole account is propaganda created by the Troyes Fraternity. Certainly there are inconsistencies within his recounting of events that are not reconcilable with known facts. More importantly, there are some possibly telling omissions that make Guillaume's work even more suspect.

Guillaume tells us that in 1118 (1119 in some versions of the document), a small group of nine knights left France and set out for the Holy Land. Their avowed intention was to form a religious brotherhood, the purpose of which was to guard the roads between the coast of the Levant and Jerusalem in order to make them safe for the many pilgrims who had chosen to make their way there after the Holy City was secured.

The leader of the nine knights was a man by the name of Hugh de Payens. It is known that Hugh was a man who held lands in northwest Troyes from his liege lord, and almost certainly his kinsman, Hugh, Count of Champagne. Some of the other original knights are named and though few of them appear again in history to any great extent, they tend to be minor nobles from Champagne, Burgundy or Flanders. One is of particular interest because he is listed as being André de Montbard who, as we have seen, was the uncle of Bernard of Clairvaux.

Arriving in Jerusalem, footsore, dirty and weary, the little band immediately made its way to the palace of the king of Jerusalem. Here we have something of a problem, because Guillaume simply refers to the king in question as being Baudoin. The complication arises from the fact that there were two Baudoins, the first being the brother of Godfroi de Bouillon, who reigned until 1119. Assuming that the tale has any real truth about it, we might expect that it was this king that was approached by Hugh de Payens and his comrades, though it is just as likely to have been Baudoin II, cousin of the child-less Baudoin I.

According to the story, the knights were received cordially and Baudoin applauded their intentions. Without further ado, he lodged them in the old stables adjoining his palace on the

Temple Mount, in the immediate vicinity of the earlier Jewish temples that had adorned the site. The stables were, by contemporary accounts, extremely large and well-apportioned buildings capable of housing literally hundreds of horses. The stables were a wing of Baudoin's own palace and, by the standards of the day, would have represented comfortable and highly desirable accommodation.

This, in essence, is the some total of our knowledge of nine years, during which time we knew nothing of what the Templar knights were doing. There is not a single other contemporary record that shows them engaged in the very activity for which they had supposedly been formed and, as far as we know, they did not appoint any new members to their order until they returned to France around 1127. This period (the missing nine years) has been the foundation of more speculation on the part of writers than just about any other subject in medieval history.

Some of this speculation asserts that the knights spent the missing years digging below the stables where they were housed, into the very heart of the ruins of Herod's and ultimately Solomon's temples. There, it has been suggested, they discovered everything from the Ark of the Covenant to the head of Jesus himself. There is absolutely no independent proof of any of this and the simple truth is that we just do not know what Hugh de Payens and his colleagues were doing during this period. Interested readers might wish to review the ideas of Baigent, Leigh and Lincoln in *The Holy Blood and the Holy Grail* and perhaps the work of Knight and Lomas in *The Hiram Key* for two interesting and different views on the lost years. Though we find interest in both these works, we are still faced with the fact that the information they contain cannot be verified by any hard evidence.

It is, however, perhaps worth mentioning at this juncture the particular ideas of Knight and Lomas. It is their assertion, in *The Hiram Key,* that the original Templar knights came across documents which they knew to have been hidden in the many secret passages beneath the old Temple since AD 70. Much more recently, amongst the documents found at Qumran, was a copper scroll that gave a list of other scrolls that had been secreted in Jerusalem below the Temple. Of course, this list did not come to light until the twentieth century, but it is conceivable that other such lists existed, that one had surfaced in the intervening period and that it had somehow come into the possession of the Troyes Fraternity. We even have to face the possibility that knowledge of the Jerusalem cache had been passed from the Essene down the Druidic/Culdean line, suggesting that a particular group of initiates would have known where to look for the hidden documents. This, essentially, is what Knight and Lomas suggest. We do not find any great fault with this assertion. In fact, to some extent it makes great sense, but it does have one major flaw, this being the time-scale.

From the very start, we had been only too aware of the great similarities between the nature and composition of the Essene and that of the much later Cistercians. We itemized these similarities in chapter 3. Further to this, we have discussed the War Rule Scroll of the Essene, in which particular instructions were given for the composition, behaviour and dress of an army that would fight a subsequent battle (against forces that could have been seen as temporal or spiritual). Whether or not the original Templar knights did spend their time looking for other hidden documents beneath the Temple Mound in Jerusalem, it is likely that they already possessed at least some documentation from the period of the Jewish revolt.

Included amongst the material in their possession, are likely to have been documents known as the War Rule Scroll and also the "Book of Jubilees". These we estimate, would have given the Troyes Fraternity the necessary impetus and information to found an order such as the Cistercians, which so closely mirrored the Essene communities. The War Rule Scroll is the most likely document to have prompted the Troyes Fraternity into forming an armed monastic order as an offshoot of the Cistercians.

Any such historical material, even though accepted and revered by the agencies in question, could only be utilized in a way that fitted neatly into the patterns of society prevailing at the time (but the parallels remain startling nevertheless). As to where the Troyes Fraternity could have come by such evidence, there is probably little mystery. As we have suggested, even today, under conditions of the most extreme archaeological security, it is still possible to buy ancient manuscripts of many sorts on the black market in and around Jerusalem. Prior to the First Crusade, Christians were by no means prohibited from visiting the Holy City. If Arab shepherds could chance upon secreted documents in the twentieth century, there is no reason why this could not have also been the case in the tenth or eleventh centuries. We also have to face the possibilities that the ruling agencies in Burgundy, or members of one of the most active Salt Line families, had possessed such documents for many centuries.

We conclude that it is almost inevitable that we will never know for certain how such Essene documents came into the possession of those agencies that underpinned the foundation of the Cistercians and the Templars. However, we have no doubt that, by one means or another, they had acquired this material.

Perhaps, the best way to view the possible actions of Hugh de Payens and his little band is to take a look at what was happening back in Champagne at the time and to reflect on our earlier comments regarding the general political and religious complexion of the Western world during the period in question.

It seems fairly clear to us that, in a basically two-pronged strategy such as that adopted by the Troyes Fraternity, it would have been vital to have the necessary infrastructure in place in the far west before the Knights Templar could be instituted as an order (without raising the suspicions of various kings and potentates). This in itself may go some way towards explaining the delay. It will be recalled that St Bernard of Clairvaux entered the Cistercian order in 1113, at which time he was twenty-three years of age. He had clearly been chosen as the brightest representative of one of the most important families in the Troyes Fraternity, but it took time for him to gain power and influence within the Cistercian movement and Christian circles as a whole. The contemplation of an order of fighting monks was new, unique and original, and it might take some persuasion to get the Vatican, in particular, to accept the notion.

There were already Templar-type institutions in existence at the time. In particular, there was the Knights of St John, otherwise known as the Hospitallers. This institution was the logical extension of a hospital, which had been founded for Christians in Jerusalem even before the crusade. As an order, the Hospitallers were not officially recognized until 1113 when Paschal II formalized them into an order. It eventually became not only an institution for tending the sick, but also a capable, and even formidable fighting force, that waged war against the forces of Islam. However, fighting was not the original remit of the order and, in this form, the Hospitallers were perhaps somewhat later than the Templars and may even have drawn inspiration from Templar ideas.

By the time the Templar knights were received back in France, at the Council of Troyes in 1128, the pope was Honorius II. Bernard of Clairvaux was thirty-eight years of age and was perhaps the most powerful man in Christendom, with the possible exception of the pope himself. Bernard was not the nominal head of the Cistercian movement, for that position was vested in the abbot of Citeaux, but nobody doubts that the position would have been his had he so desired it. In reality, the very fact that Bernard never chose to be abbot of Citeaux or pope is the strongest indication that he was well aware of the fact that his energies were to be exploited in other directions. Freed from the political and administrative minefield that both these elevated positions carried, Bernard could then be the "power behind all thrones". Although Bernard wasn't the head of the Cistercians, he was its greatest leading light; leader, in all but name, of the greatest single monastic institution the world had ever seen. By 1128, men were flocking into the Cistercian

houses from all parts of the Christian world, and in unprece-
dented numbers. It was a ground swell of public opinion and
popularity that no pope could ignore, and especially not the
beleaguered Honorius II, a man replete with problems and
surrounded by enemies.

Bernard probably spent some time persuading Honorius that
the existence of the Templars could only serve as a bastion for
the independence of the Holy See. In any case, such was the
power of Bernard and his movement by this date, it is hard to
see how any pope could have refused the request.

Of course, this doesn't directly answer the question of what
the nine original Templar knights had been doing with
themselves for nine years in Jerusalem. Perhaps, as we have
suggested, they had been digging beneath the floor of the
stables, intent on finding something (or perhaps anything) in the
ruins of the old temples, but it is just as likely that they were
busy consolidating their position and making important new
friends in and around Jerusalem. In truth, there isn't any hard
evidence that all nine knights remained in the area across the
whole nine years. Knowing the logistical nightmare that would
face Hugh de Payens as first grand master of the Templar order,
it is very unlikely that he would have kicked his heels in
Jerusalem for so long.

Certainly there does seem to be tentative evidence of much
coming and going between the Levant and Champagne during
the period. It is a fact that whilst the Templar founders were in
Jerusalem, Bernard of Clairvaux had been making his abbey
into a resort for esoteric study. Rather strangely, for such a
deeply Christian foundation, Bernard had acquired the skills of
certain Jewish scholars who were ensconced within the abbey
itself. Since it is our contention that the Troyes Fraternity was
well aware of its archaic roots, and that it also knew there were
old Jewish connections within the earliest Culdean Christianity,
we feel empowered to speculate with regard to Bernard's
actions.

It was widely held in Christendom that there was some great

secret associated with Solomon's Temple. Indeed this belief did not subside with the passing of time, for even much later in the seventeenth century Sir Isaac Newton, father of science, was absolutely obsessed with the notion and is known to have penned several million words on the subject. The whole thrust of the Troyes Fraternity was geared towards the "New Jerusalem", which had also been a topic of some interest to the much earlier St Augustine, for whom Bernard showed the greatest reverence. Many of the most secret and esoteric beliefs that seem to have been endemic to the inner circles of Cistercianism, and to the Templar movement, only became known when they were later translated into Rosicrucianism and Freemasonry, but few doubt that they were present even in Bernard's time.

Following back from the revelations of these later institutions, which we shall soon look at more closely, it would appear that Bernard, and therefore by implication the Troyes Fraternity, had a particular fascination for the Cabala, the esoteric and magical traditions of the Jews. From this interest would arise the fanatical western European obsession with alchemy, which may already have been present as a subject for study in the darkest recesses of Clairvaux abbey. We envisage a situation in which Hugh de Payens and his colleagues wandered the bazaars and markets of Jerusalem, voraciously pawing over the many fragments of documents, which still come to light in the city to this day, and of course we cannot rule out the possibility that they unearthed more themselves.

Anything of interest would have been sent back to Clairvaux, where it would have been translated by Bernard's scholars, men seasoned in the reading of Greek, Latin, Hebrew and Aramaic. Were the Templars looking for something specific? Was there some previous clue that led them to documents of practical or simply historical worth? The best we can say at this distance is that there is insufficient evidence to be certain. But even if the answer to this question were to be "no", this does not mean that the collection of almost any ancient documents would have represented a futile exercise. In order to explore this assumption, we need to take a look at some of the skills that seem to have been endemic to the Templar order from the very date of its official formation in 1128.

The Templars were great sailors. During the period of time that the order existed it sent ships all over the known world, sometimes undertaking frighteningly long journeys on a very regular basis. The Templars explored the Black Sea, knew the Baltic and may have sailed around large parts of Africa. They were familiar with the seas around Britain, had certainly visited Orkney and the Shetlands, probably travelled to Iceland and, most staggering of all, almost certainly knew of the Americas.

The skills necessary to undertake these journeys were not acquired overnight. It is quite possible that they were assisted by documents and maps that ultimately derived from Arab sources, or from Egyptian documents held amongst Jewish texts hidden deep within the catacombs of the old Temple. The Templars could have learned much about advanced geometry and mathematics from other Jewish documents obtained back in the days of the Temple from Jewish, Hellenistic and Alexandrian sources.

Such documents may also account for another skill that seems to have been instantly obvious to the Templars after their official formation, namely the handling of architectural techniques. By the time of the rise of the Templars, the Cistercians were already developing their own simple styles of building. These are paled into insignificance by the achievements of both orders subsequently. It is a fact that the most elegant and clever architectural building style of the period, Gothic, suddenly emerged in western Europe at exactly the time that the Templars were putting the first stages of their business empire together. We would not be the first writers to suggest that the Gothic style, with its high thin walls and stress-levelling flying buttresses, originated in the comprehension of talented Templar builders, who used these and other techniques in their own churches and fantastic castles.

The Templars became adept at many aspects of farming and animal husbandry. They constructed farm buildings that were revolutionary in their day and understood the complexities of working with water-power for mills. Like the Cistercians, they were extremely clever at utilizing water supplies in ways that had not been seen in Europe previously. Moving entire rivers to facilitate better sanitary conditions within their various establishments, they created clean, hygienic hospitals for the old and wounded, and were leading lights in the provision of water closets and inbuilt sanitation. The Templars were expert financiers, using trading techniques quite unknown in the Europe of their day. They had clearly learned many of these skills from Jewish sources, but would have much more freedom to extend their financial empire in a way that any Jewish financier of the period would have envied greatly.

Nor should we ignore the apparent fascination that the Templars had for magic. We can laugh at such concepts today, but by the standards of the twelfth century, the study was truly valid and probably extremely useful. Excursions into the Cabala and experiments with alchemy ultimately led to all manner of chemical processes that would prove to be a boon to the dawning of science. The Templars stood at the very threshold of these matters.

If the order was to flourish and grow quickly after its initial acceptance by the pope, it would be necessary to have all these skills honed to perfection. With these considerations in mind, we can see that the original nine Templar knights, during the time they spent in the Holy Land, probably enjoyed scarcely a moment to themselves. Undoubtedly, they had travelled to Jerusalem with a particular set of instructions, and the sudden and staggering success of the post 1128 Templars shows that they had not been lax in their quest for knowledge, no matter from whence it came.

Accusations levelled at the Templars at the time of the trials in the fourteenth century, together with information which passed via them to Freemasonry, show the Templars to have amassed swathes of ancient knowledge, not only from the Levant itself, but also from Egyptian sources. All of this undoubtedly consolidated the existing ancient knowledge held by the Troyes Fraternity, for these people had been for countless centuries the wise men and magicians of their people. These arts were also turned to the direction for which the Templars are most famous: fighting. They learned how to deploy forces in ways unknown to Western strategists and gained knowledge of fighting in the vastly different climate and terrain of the Middle East. In addition, they studied the knowledge of Turkish and Arab leaders, thus evolving new siege machines and learning how to make their bastions virtually impregnable to attack.

All of this and more was the initial work of only nine men. Not surprisingly, we are left with the impression that, rather than wondering what they were actually doing for a mere nine years, it is incredible that they were ready in under ninety years. Doubtless the Templars learned much along the way, but if the order was going to survive and flourish from the word go, its leadership would have to be knowledgeable, competent and sure-footed.

When the call came, they made their way back to Troyes. Bronzed and hardened by the harsh glare of the eastern sun, they received the white garb of their order and the written constitution that Bernard of Clairvaux had so painstakingly created for them. They rode in triumph through the city and then began a processional that would last for many months. Before the decade was over, the adventure was underway, and no loss or adversity would halt its relentless pace for the next two centuries; in fact it has never been entirely diminished to the present day.

Chapter 16

Triumph

In our previous book, *The Warriors and the Bankers*, we attempted to demonstrate the true nature of the Templar movement as it flourished and grew both within Europe and much further afield in the Holy Land. However, it will be necessary for the sake of readers who do not have access to our previous work to look again at the development of what may be the most remarkable phenomenon that Europe ever knew.

Many historians, when discussing the Templars, have attempted to demonstrate ways in which the order "evolved" in those years following its acceptance at the Council of Troyes. However, to suggest that Templar motivations and plans altered during the order's earliest years might be something of a misreading. A dispassionate look at the rise of the Templars between the beginning of the twelfth century and the end of the thirteenth century proves conclusively that it moved forward on all fronts simultaneously, conforming to a carefully laid set of plans that must have been in place from the word go. True, the institution's ability to put all its strategies in place immediately was hampered by the need to establish the logistical and financial framework it would ultimately need, but its phenomenal rate of growth soon took care of such matters. Cheek by jowl with its brother order, the Cistercians, the Templars used a number of methods to increase its size and power in the shortest time possible.

The avowed intention of the Templar order was to fight non-Christians and to secure forever the Holy Land for Christian posterity. It is therefore suggested, by some researchers, that all other actions taken by the Templars were peripheral to this specific requirement. Our research indicates that this was not the case and that, in fact, the possession of the Holy Land, rather than being the most important Templar *raison d'être*, was itself simply only one part of the original strategy.

The Holy Land was certainly the issue uppermost in the mind of the European public and probably also in the minds of most low-ranking Templar operatives. It was logical, at least to the brains behind the order, that if the Templars were to remain self-sufficient, and at the same time keep a large standing army in the Levant, the order would have to raise large sums of money. The financial constraints of training, equipping, transporting and servicing a large, mounted fighting force must have been truly prohibitive, especially at first. No institution that failed to make provision for the frightening fiscal consequences of such an adventure would have survived long in any age (and the agencies running the Templar order were more than aware of these facts).

Meaningful research regarding the year-by-year growth of the Templar order is difficult, if not impossible. There is one specific reason for this state of affairs. From beginning to end, the Templar order was shot through with secrecy. This was a deliberate policy on the part of the Templar founding fathers, and they must have realized very early that the very nature of their enterprise made its true size and shape virtually impossible for outsiders to ascertain.

In the case of the Cistercians, anyone could see the tangible reality of an abbey (such an edifice could hardly be hidden), no matter how remote many of the Cistercian foundations may have been. Any monarch wishing to assess the wealth of the

Cistercian houses within his domains could quite easily send out agents to assess the value of lands, count the number of sheep and cattle, and value the abbeys themselves. To this extent, the Cistercians were likely, when their wealth grew beyond a certain point, to find themselves criticized, particularly since they were not subject to taxes and tithes in the way other institutions and individuals were. In fact, this was often the case and the agencies that levelled such criticism at least had facts and figures at their fingertips.

Although the Templars attracted critical attention, and in the end far more than the Cistercians, it was often based on a degree of supposition that was inevitable simply because the scale of the Templar empire was completely unknown. Templar properties such as farms, churches, villages, ports and headquarters, could be counted as readily as the monasteries of the Cistercians. But from the very start of the institution, there were so many variables that to see the larger picture would have been impossible for any single monarch. So widespread was the Templar wealth, so diffuse the elements that supported it, that only in conclave, and after some very careful and hard-won calculations, could the collective monarchs of Europe have been privy to something like the full extent of Templar holdings. The agencies behind the formation of the Templars were well aware of this and fully exploited the fact that there was very little tangible cohesion between thrones in the region. In this, as in many other things, they showed a genius quite beyond the capabilities of the monarchs within whose domains they flourished.

We are entitled to ask: "From where did the initial financial impetus to even commence the Templar empire come?" The nine knights who attended the Troyes gathering of 1128 were, according to orthodox accounts, "poor". In fact, this was reflected in the name chosen for the order because they were the "Poor Knights of Christ and the Temple of Solomon". Nothing could be further from the truth, for even if the founder knights themselves were not of middle-ranking aristocratic stock (which most of them certainly were), they had extremely rich backers, not the least of whom was the fabulously rich Hugh, Count of Champagne. But all the money in Champagne could not have financed the exploits of the Templars on the field of battle alone.

Ultimately people flocked to offer gifts to the Templars. Aristocratic families gave parcels of land, fallen soldiers left their entire estates, and kings even split their domains in order to feed the voracious appetite of the soldiers abroad. But this was certainly not the case in 1128. If the Troyes Fraternity was to see its plans mature successfully, it was necessary to get as many well-trained fighters into the Levant as quickly as was humanly possible. Political cohesion across Europe was weak; in fact it was something of a miracle that the First Crusade had ever happened at all. As history would eventually show, to expect to maintain a successful hold on so much land, so far from western Europe, could never depend entirely on the goodwill of disparate and often warring monarchs. This was part of the reason that something akin to the Templars simply had to exist.

What was needed was a quick-start mechanism by which the Templars could be up and functioning in the shortest time possible. This was achieved by the Troyes Fraternity through mobilizing members of its own conclave from far and wide. We offer two examples of this policy at work at the very commencement of the order, though there were undoubtedly many other examples.

First of all, the order was given large areas of land in Troyes itself. Hugh de Champagne, who was eventually open in admitting his Templar connections by actually becoming a Templar knight, offered a base and a home to the Templars within his own Troyes Salt Line domains. The earliest Templars also had holdings to the north and west of the city, donated by Hugh de Payens, the first grand master of the order.

The second example is even more interesting, simply because it is more telling. Supposedly Hugh de Payens was married at the time the Templars were first formed. This in itself is rather strange, since celibacy was a prerequisite for all Templars. His wife is said to have been of the family of St Clair, and it was via this connection that the first Templar property outside of France and the Holy Land came to exist.

The St Clairs, later the Sinclairs, owned land to the south of Edinburgh in Scotland and a large parcel of this land passed into the hands of the Templars immediately after the Council of Troyes in 1128. The St Clairs and Sinclairs were to prove pivotal to Templar and post-Templar history for many centuries, but what is most striking about this family is their point of origin. The St Clairs rose to prosperity in Normandy, in a place called Pont L'Eveque. Pont L'Eveque is situated firmly on a longitudinal Salt Line. The behaviour of this family, both at this time and subsequently, demonstrates that they were quite clearly of one mind with the Troyes Fraternity and that they may even have been directly involved in the developing stages of the whole imperative.

Apart from mobilizing support from the old Salt Line families of western Europe, the Templar organizers had another card up their sleeve. They were, particularly after the Council of Troyes, a fully sanctioned religious order of monks. It was therefore appropriate to write into the rule a proviso that any individual joining the order must surrender all his possessions at the time of entry, and if he was a member of the landowning aristocracy this also related to his manorial holdings.

Although virtually impossible to prove, it is also highly likely that the Templars received initial support, possibly in cash but almost certainly in kind, from the Cistercians with whom they were so intimately associated.

Within only a few short years of their official creation, the Templar order had lands in practically every area of western Europe and far beyond. The more prominent they became, the greater was their popularity and the more they attracted new benefactors and recruits.

To those who had carefully planned the rapid growth of

Templarism, to build a widespread but cohesive infrastructure as quickly as possible was important for reasons other than the initial wealth it provided. It was also the means by which the monastic order could become a company of "merchant adventurers". It wasn't very long before the succession of grand Templar preceptories throughout the more populous cites of Europe and beyond provided the means to build the banking institution, which was to become one of the primary legacies of Templarism.

Travel in the twelfth century was extremely dangerous. Bandits occupied every forest and even controlled many towns and villages. It was therefore perilous enough to get oneself safely from one part of the region to another, let alone to consider transporting large amounts of money that were necessary for trade and commerce to flourish. The Templars solved this problem at a stroke, by instituting a form of cheque-book banking. In principle, this was very simple. For example, a merchant from Bristol in England who wanted to undertake a financial transaction in Paris would simply deposit a prescribed sum of money in the Templar establishment in his own town. In exchange for the money, he would be supplied with a promissory note written in cipher – an item that would have been of no use to a potential robber. Our merchant would then travel to Paris, unencumbered by the cash, and go immediately to the Templar headquarters in the city. On production of the note, and proof of his identity, he would be given his money in the local currency, less (and this is the most important fact) a handling fee. The fee was not large – certainly a good investment in terms of insurance for the safe arrival of the money – and it was proportional to the amount in question. Thus the merchant was happy and a little more profit passed into the coffers of the Templar order.

Such transactions did not break the ecclesiastical law of the time which forbade Christians from receiving interest on loans made to other Christians, because the shortfall on the merchant's deposit could be accounted for in a number of different ways, for example, fluctuating exchange rates.

Actually, the Templars did eventually come to openly charge interest on the many loans they made, but by this stage they were so powerful that there was little anyone could do about the situation.

One of the basic tenets of our previous research has been to treat the Templar enterprise as if it represented a large, multinational company (which we slightly irreverently referred to as Templar Inc.). Amongst our readers, this proved to be very popular, simply because it can be shown to be an accurate assessment of the situation. Like any good, modern, multinational, Templar Inc. did not restrict itself to any one activity. This was a mistake the Cistercians were to make to their great cost and also possibly to the chagrin of the Templars, though even the Cistercians did not have problems with over-specialization for nearly two centuries. One of the Templars most important "subsidiaries" was its shipping arm.

The Templars great seafaring skills are legendary. The mathematical knowledge that underpinned this maritime success was almost certainly part of an ancient legacy, as we shall presently see, but its practical applications were exploited to the full. During Christian possession of the Holy Land, or parts of it, the Templars had virtually sole rights to passenger shipping, plying the routes between the seaports of western Europe and those of the Levant. Pilgrims felt safe from piracy with armed Templar knights to guard them and so business was very good. But the Templars also created a large merchant fleet, plying the same routes. Outgoing goods would include the necessary Western requisites for the growing European elite in the Levant, together with the Templar's own garrison requirements. Homeward bound, there was no lack of cargoes. All manner of merchandise, readily available in the Middle East, was of the greatest interest to western Europe. Spices, exotic woods, acquired Turkish and Jewish treasure, new and rare plant species, all filled the holds of Templar merchantmen that frequented the busy wharves of southern and eastern France during the eleventh century.

It may have been the explicit desire of the Troyes Fraternity to undermine the power of State and Church in the Europe of their day, but it seems they did not fight shy of a little "self help" that became possible on the way. We refer specifically to the formation of the "Champagne fairs" which sprang up as a direct response to the increased trade traffic between Europe, the Mediterranean and the Middle East. The Troyes region of Champagne, because of its geographical position, had probably always been a centre of trade and exchange. However, with the capture of the Holy Land, the small and casual markets of the region gave way to much more formalized and better-ordered varieties, which became the very lifeblood of national and inter-national trade. Ultimately, there were six Champagne fairs, or markets, held in the region annually. The town of Lagne sported one, as did Bar-sur-Aube. Provins, the great rose-growing area, and Troyes itself each ran two fairs per year. The duration of each fair was forty-nine days. The purpose of the fair was to exchange cloth, brought down in the main from Flanders, for the many commodities to be had from further south and from abroad.

One peculiarity of these fairs was the use of letters that promised full payment of a particular debt at the next fair. In this respect, the fairs showed the first appearance in Europe of the use of credit transactions. It is hard to believe that such practices had not been introduced by the Templars, or more likely by the institution that stood behind the Templar order. It is also certain that the Templars gained a great deal from the fairs either by acting through agents as suppliers of merchan-dise, or as shippers and transporters of the various goods on offer.

The Champagne fairs carried on, in one form or another, well into the fourteenth century, but all experts agree that their primary importance had waned by the beginning of the fourteenth century. In other words, the period of the great success of the Champagne fairs exactly matched that of the Templar order itself. With the demise of the Templars as an official institution, trade patterns changed, as we will show in due course.

It might be instructive to take a closer look at the way the Champagne fairs were guaranteed to benefit not only the Templar order itself, but also the growing number of abbeys in the Cistercian family. When the true picture is seen, it becomes impossible to believe that the whole structure developed entirely by fortuitous chance. The Champagne fairs, all of which were to be found in the same region, and two of which took place annually in Troyes itself, had been specifically created with one major proviso in mind; namely, the shifting of large quantities of finished woollen cloth throughout Europe and beyond. We have already seen that the greatest sheep farmers in Europe by the thirteenth century were the Cistercians, who were running massive herds at most of their larger abbey sites. But this lucrative farming opportunity was not lost on the Templars either, and many of the larger Templar farms were themselves raising sizeable herds of sheep.

Sheep proved to be a fantastic investment to both orders, which capitalized on the asset very early in their history by constantly improving the breeds and by also adding "clover", the rough pasture upon which sheep can perfectly well manage to survive. It is quite likely that the whole Cistercian order was written with sheep in mind, since the order was committed to self-sufficiency in "desert" regions as far from other human habitation as possible. Although the Cistercians were capable cattle farmers, it was the sheep that first exploited the poor land upon which most Cistercian abbeys were founded.

Sheep proved to be "gold on legs" for the Cistercians and the Templars. Later, we shall itemize a famous post-Templar order called the Order of the Golden Fleece. In fact, this is a sort of literary pun, despite its archaic allusions. The creation of such wealth, culled from the most marginal land imaginable by the simple expedient of cutting back the scrub and putting sheep on the land, was an "alchemy" of a sort, and particularly so once the right merchant structures were put in place.

Virtually all Cistercian wool, and especially that from both Britain and northern France, ultimately found its way to the area around the city of Bruges, in what is today Belgium. There, the local populace were skilled at rapidly turning the wool into cloth, and it was this cloth that was brought to the Champagne fairs. We can therefore clearly see how important these fairs were to the Cistercians and the Templars. The Cistercians' ultimate wealth derived in great part from the wool and, to a lesser degree, the same was true of the Templars. But Templarism took the matter several stages further. Templar money was involved in the financial transactions at every stage, and it is quite likely that they were also responsible for transhipping much of the wool to the ports of Flanders. They also held most of the monopolies on the other end of the trade; namely the vast quantity of desirable merchandise finding its way to Champagne from the Levant, North Africa and the Mediterranean area in general. At every single stage, the Templars were deriving more and more revenue, some of which was used to build larger merchant fleets and to consolidate the banking empire that was being established.

The planning that went into creating Templar Inc. shows an understanding of the various components of commerce that would have absolutely baffled most people during the period during which it took place. Before a puzzled and wholly outclassed series of monarchs across Europe and beyond could react, the whole business empire was up and running. Indeed, there is much reason to believe that most of the monarchs whose kingdoms participated in this trade would have been very happy to see the status quo maintained and strengthened, since they were able to levy taxes, as English monarchs were to do with regard to the woollen exports. This is yet another example of how the Troyes Fraternity turned the natural greed inherent within the ruling classes of the western European feudal systems to its own ends.

Both the Cistercians and the Templars had a head start on most other institutions of a more temporal nature in that they were not faced with prohibitive wage bills for their workers. Monks and Templars alike had to be fed and clothed, and adequately provisioned to carry on their allotted professions, but they were not paid one groat. Consequently, practically all the profit made on the business transactions was reinvested to make even more money later. It was a situation that any modern business co-operation would be forced to envy.

The Templars eventually became so rich that the monarchs of some of the kingdoms within which they operated were wholly dependent on their support. Several kings of England actually lodged the treasury of the realm at the Templar headquarters in London, as surety against the massive debts they ran up with the order. This gave the Templars great power to influence decision-making, and they regularly acted as arbiters for warring monarchs.

Arm in arm, the Templars and their brothers the Cistercians walked on confidently into the twelfth and thirteenth centuries. The triumphs and reversals of the Templars as a fighting force is the story of another chapter, though none of the subsequent defeats in battle seem to have affected adversely their economic success. For about sixteen decades, neither order experienced any real financial problems whatsoever, and so were able to capitalize on their early success and strengthen the infrastructure of both orders. Only towards the end of the thirteenth century did the over-specialization of the Cistercians nearly land them hot water. Even the Templars, by this period rich beyond the dreams of any temporal monarch, were not immune to the consequences.

Chapter 17

The Seeds of Disaster

The suggestion is made by Baigent, Leigh and Lincoln in *The Holy Blood and the Holy Grail* that there was a definite historical split between the Templar order and the body that had been responsible for its origins, an institution which they refer to as the Order of Sion. Supposedly, this came about because of Templar ineptitude at the time Jerusalem fell to the Saracens in 1187. Whether or not the Templars were responsible for the loss of Jerusalem has always been a matter of great debate. We would suggest that true to the struggles that had taken place for nearly a century in the region, even the might of the Templars could not hope to retain the Holy City without the full co-operation of other agencies. This assistance was frequently and pointedly not forthcoming. It is therefore likely that the Templars, already under verbal attack from many quarters at the time Jerusalem was lost, were used as a convenient scapegoat for the loss of city.

It does follow, however, that if there was a continued presence of the Troyes Fraternity in Jerusalem (i.e. the Order of Sion), it would have been forced to retire in 1187, either to a more secure area of the Levant or back to Europe.

The mysterious Prieure de Sion, from whom Baigent, Leigh

and Lincoln received their information regarding the split between the Templars and the Order of Sion, indicated that it took place in the northern French town of Gisors in 1188. The documents made available to Baigent, Leigh and Lincoln refer to this formalized severing of cordial relations as "The Cutting of the Elm". What little is historically known about events in Gisors in 1188 refers to a meeting held there between Philip II of France and Henry II of England. The Prieure de Sion document dealing with this incident is not specific as to what actually happened in, or rather just outside, the fortified town, but historical accounts talk in a garbled way about some disagreement regarding an elm tree. The French eventually chopped down this tree. In reality, this is probably the only memorable event in an otherwise abortive meeting between two monarchs who were regularly at odds with each other.

There certainly does not appear to be any direct evidence to suggest that the erstwhile mentors of the Templars suddenly chose to cast the order adrift. Had they chosen to do so, it is difficult to see how it could possibly have had any real bearing on the Templar order, which even in its formal and approved status still had well over a century to run. By this stage of history, the Templars could possibly boast at least 20,000 knights in its ranks. As we have seen, the knights represented the backbone of the institution. For every mounted fighter, there were probably eight or ten other men whose functions were less glamorous but equally necessary. This would mean that the Templar order comprised at least 160,000 members, a great percentage of whom were specifically dedicated to mercantile and maritime operations. Any organization on this scale, and which held half the crowned heads of a continent in its economic hands, was hardly likely to take too much notice of any other temporal or spiritual authority. It had, by this stage, become a huge machine and one that responded principally to its own needs. It was this aspect of Templar Inc. that monarchs such as Philip IV feared so much and why, ultimately, attempts had to be made to dismantle it.

However, for the moment, even with the loss of Jerusalem, the Templars were secure and we can personally find no evidence that the structure of the order underwent any radical change at this time. The fortunes of the Christians in the Levant gradually worsened throughout the end of the twelfth century and much of the thirteenth. Templar knights had garrisons in just about every town and city in occupied Judea, and in many locations beyond it. History shows that they fought tenaciously for every scrap of land to which they had been sent, and that their basic motivation to fight those who would persecute Christians remained intact until the West was forced to withdraw entirely from the Levant.

There is no hard evidence that relations between the two factions, Cistercian and Templar, remained anything but cordial during this long period. There are regular examples of Templar knights visiting and being made welcome in Cistercian monasteries, and the common trade links remained intact. Despite persistent assertions by some agencies that the end of the twelfth century also marked some sort of split between the Cistercians and the Templars, as well as between the Templars and the Order of Sion, all the available evidence shows that such a parting of the ways did not take place until the 1280s. When it did happen, it was due to economic pressures and was almost certainly never a formal severing of relations.

The Cistercians and the Templars, two of the most influential and richest monastic institutions the world would ever know, found themselves in difficult circumstances at an identical period, though for very different reasons. The rapid change of events in the latter half of the thirteenth century must have looked to the deeply religious as if the Hand of God was meting out a justice born of the arrogance and wealth he saw displayed before him. In the case of the Cistercians, there is no doubt that the order had degenerated to a tremendous extent. During the thirteenth century, one by one the bastions upon which the order had built its success began to crumble. Originally, the brothers had been simple farmers; vegetarians dedicated to a life of hard work and constant prayer, living and worshipping in Spartan conditions. By the latter part of the thirteenth century, the Cistercians looked little different to any of the other "fat" monastic institutions of the period.

Gradually the simple, aisle-less churches of the first monasteries, specifically designed to avoid ostentatious frills and fancies, became bigger and more ornate. The tombs of wealthy patrons stuck out into the formerly barren chancels; sumptuous altars dripped with silver, gold and precious stones. Rich carvings decorated capitals and rood screens, while priests in vestments of bright colours and cloth of gold officiated over solid gold communion cups and Italian marble altar tables. As the services were called, massive bells rung out in gigantic towers in contravention of one of the most specifically forbidden architectural commandments to early Cistercian builders.

In the refectory, choir monks and lay brothers alike ate more frequently. They drank up to a gallon of beer each and every day, washing down large quantities of well-cooked meat, once anathema to everyone in the order except the aged and the sick. By 1280, the old system of two-tiered monasticism was still, but just barely, in place, but control over lay brothers in sometimes very distant granges was lax. Meanwhile, many of the choir monks had become physically idle, spending more and more time polishing the face of the church, and less and less hours in the field and the garden.

The public at large was not blind. It could see for itself what Cistercianism had become. It had been many decades since an adoring public poured unimaginable wealth into the order. As a result, much religious attention gradually turned away from the Benedictines and Cistercians, towards the "Friars" whose institutions seemed far more praiseworthy as paragons of godliness. Consequently, it was more difficult to find monks to replace those who died, especially amongst the lay brothers. But somehow the institution stayed in one piece, growing richer and more opulent with each passing day. It could hardly fail to do this, since its founding economic principles had been so meticulously thought out.

Anyone who looks carefully at the Cistercians of the later thirteenth century is almost certain to recognize an institution which had gone beyond its own zenith. It could still dispose of its limited number of young brothers with reforming zeal by sending them off to found yet more houses in the few available regions that remained, but its only real reason to survive had always been to grow. Once it was more or less impossible to increase the number of abbeys, the only other response was to spend more and more money on the foundations it already possessed, and this was the first step on the extremely long and very sad road to ruin.

If there was anything left of the order that St Stephen Harding or St Bernard of Clairvaux would recognize by around 1280, even that was soon to disappear. Paradoxically, the hammer blow was brought about by forces quite beyond the control of anyone within the order.

In the eighth decade of the thirteenth century, much of western Europe experienced a succession of extremely wet and cold years, a fact that is noted in a number of chronicles from the period. This fact alone would have made life difficult for the Cistercians, whose very livelihood still depended upon farming. What made matters worse, in fact much worse, was the onset of sheep scab, a pestilence that raced through the flocks at an alarming rate. Many of the sheep died, whilst most of the others gave extremely poor yields of wool. The weather and the disease had come like a bolt from the blue and at a time when the abbeys were nearly all in hock up to their gargoyles.

If the Cistercian houses had remained lean and simple, there would have been no problem, for they would have been sitting on large enough reserves to see them through the difficult years. The fact is that the majority of Cistercian houses, and particularly the British and northern French ones, had been paid for their wool anything up to five years in advance. They were honour bound to meet the commitments which they had made, and that meant borrowing more money to buy in extra wool to send to the merchants in Flanders.

As an example of what nearly all the wool-producing abbeys experienced, Fountains in North Yorkshire, England, saw manageable debts of £900 in 1274, rise to an unbelievable £6,373 by 1291. This seven-fold rise in debt was impossible to address without the severest tightening of belts, and this would represent millions in modern terms. In many cases, such as that of Rievaulx, practically the oldest and most venerated Cistercian house in England, independent officers appointed by the king had to be brought in to help sort matters out. The Cistercians had always been fiercely independent and had fought off the avaricious glances of generations of monarchs. The recognition that they must seek help from such a direction must have come as a bitter blow to any brothers who still revered the path of the founders.

Of course, the Cistercians were not the only ones to suffer; the weather and the sheep scab affected everyone equally. It brought repercussions that had a tremendous bearing on the Templars too, even beyond their own farming losses regarding the problem of sheep scab. It is no coincidence that this period coincides neatly with the beginning of a slow but marked decline in the power and influence of the Champagne fairs, institutions that had lain at the very heart of Templar economic success.

Even the losses incurred with this regard could probably have been more cheerfully absorbed and dealt with were in not for the fact that the area of the Levant garrisoned and controlled by Templar knights was growing smaller and smaller. The bitterest blow of all came in 1291 when the last garrison in the mainland of the Levant, "Acre", fell to the forces of Islam. The Templars there had fought with conspicuous and even fanatical bravery, but all to no end. Whereas a continued presence in the area for the last century could have led the optimistic to believe that Jerusalem would eventually be recaptured, after 1291 everyone knew that the game was up for good.

The Cistercians dealt with their problems by abandoning the

last bastion of the rule laid down by their founding fathers; they simply got rid of the lay brotherhood. Granges were rented out to secular men, who at first acted as "estate managers" for whatever abbey owned their land and later as tenants. It was a system that worked well enough to keep the order more or less running until the sixteenth century in Britain, and even slightly longer in some areas of Europe, but in every real sense Cistercianism was dead.

The Troyes Fraternity, if it still existed in any cohesive form, would have been in no position to halt the decline. The wealth of its own members must have been greatly affected by the gradual decline of the Champagne fairs, whilst patterns of rule were changing dramatically within the French region as a whole. What made matters worse was the fact that the whole of Champagne had fallen into the hands of the French crown in 1284. We see this event as being pivotal to our whole story.

Some years earlier, the title of count of Champagne had fallen into the hands of the kings of Navarre. Under their patronage, the area remained a stern adversary to the French crown, whose lands it partly encircled. It was the existence of a more or less independent Champagne that had prevented successive kings of France from rooting out disaffection to their rule from further south, even though the region nominally owed allegiance to the French throne.

Ultimately the county of Champagne devolved to Henry 1 of Navarre, who seems to have been fiercely opposed to the Capetians at every stage of his rule. Henry had a young male heir, but he was tragically and accidentally dropped over the battlements of a castle by his careless nurse whilst still a babe in arms. With no other sons as heirs, Henry I of Navarre, also Count of Champagne, had planned to marry his only daughter Joan to one of the two sons of Edward I of England, either Henry or Alphonso. King Henry died in 1274, before the marriage could be arranged. Blanche, widow of Henry of Navarre and Joan's mother, feared for the life of her daughter if a battle of succession developed for the Navarre throne.

Probably unwisely, she fled for safety to the court of King Philip III of France. Such a situation could not have suited the French crown better because an alliance between France and Navarre would also bring Champagne, which French kings for generations had been attempting to subdue. It seems that significant pressure was put upon Blanche to allow a betrothal between her daughter Joan and Philip III's son, who eventually became Philip IV, the scourge of the Templars.

This wasn't quite the end of the story because Edmond, brother of Edward I of England, wooed and married Blanche, Joan of Navarre's mother. For some years Edmond and Blanche ruled Champagne, while Joan was in her minority. By the time she was twelve years of age, the French began to put pressure on Edmond and Blanche for the return of Champagne. As time passed these claims became difficult to counter. Edward I of England was unwilling to support Edmond's claim to Champagne, mainly because he was so committed to his wars in Wales. In any case, to do so would have meant war with France, and this was something the almost habitually impoverished Edward I was anxious to avoid.

In the end a compromise was reached, and it was probably the worst of all compromises for the Templars. Edmond and Blanche relinquished any further claim to Champagne in return for the sum of 60,000 livres and a dower of five Castillions. This incredible sum reflects just how badly France wished to control Champagne, the more so when it is borne in mind that Edmond and Blanche had no real right to retain the county in any case. With the celebration of Philip's marriage to Joan of Navarre in 1284, the fiercely independent Champagne disappeared forever. It is our profound belief that on the day this marriage was solemnized, the writing was on the wall for the Knights Templar in France.

The Templars were, by this time, a truly international institution and they were especially well represented in France. Their largest presbytery of all was in Paris itself, functioning right under the noses of the French crown. But the spiritual heartland of Templarism remained Champagne and, in particular, the city of Troyes. This was their official headquarters in Europe and it is entirely likely that, up to 1284, it remained the seat of that august body that had created both it and the Cistercian order some two-and-a-half centuries earlier. If the Troyes Fraternity was still functioning undisturbed in Troyes in 1284, it could not afford to do so for one moment longer. As we shall presently see, there is evidence that it almost certainly moved its base of operations around this time.

Philip IV became king of France in 1285, just one year after Champagne was ceded to France by Edmond of England and Blanche of Navarre. Philip was only seventeen years of age and inherited a kingdom replete with debt, most of which was incurred by his father, Philip III, who had spent most of his reign indulging in expensive and generally abortive wars. Any kingdom short of cash had formerly been a haven for the Templars, who were already fabulously rich and whose European properties revolved around those that now fell within the French domains. They simply lent monarchs of such states so much money that they (the Templars) invariably ended up in a position to call the political tune.

Philip was tall, handsome, athletic and fair-haired, all of which conspired to earn him the name of "Philip le Bel" ("Philip the Fair"). Philip's beauty of form was not reflected in his personality, a fact that might not have been entirely of his own making. The life of a medieval prince was probably never easy, but in Philip's case it was worse than average. Having lost his mother whilst he was still an infant, his father later remarried a beautiful but ambitious woman by the name of Marie de Brabant, after which time rumours of intrigues and possible poisoning became the order of each terrifying day at court. Philip grew to be suspicious, had a clearly defined sense of right and wrong (which involved Philip always being on the "right" side), and was possessed of a cruel streak which would have made him the envy of any medieval despot.

By the time Philip IV made up his mind that the Knights

Templar would have to go, he was thirty-nine years of age, and he had already been king of France for twenty-two years. We can be fairly sure that a decision of this magnitude was not taken lightly, and it is also certain that he ruminated about it for a considerable period before any plan was put into operation. Before we look carefully at the reasons for Philip's decision, it might be prudent to point to some of the less favourable accusations that were being levelled at the Templars, not just in France, but also in other European countries contemporary with the commencement of the fourteenth century.

It is important to eliminate remarks which are known to have been made in the years after the 1307 attack and the subsequent outlawing of the Templars by the pope. As far as we can ascertain, none of the charges subsequently levelled by Philip had ever been directly or indirectly levelled at the Templars previously. The Templars were regularly accused of arrogance, though it is hard to see how they could possibly have held their own against the bluff barons and tyrannical monarchs of the period if they had not been sure of themselves and their institution. Ordinary people had their own reasons for disliking the Templars, and this was a direct response to the sort of services they were willing to provide.

Quite often the Templars were employed as tax collectors for and on behalf of monarchs or, indeed, feudal lords. It was suggested that they were often not too particular about the methods they used to get what was due to their employers and a little extra for their own coffers. It was also stated that the Templars, declaring their intention to secure rights of passage for travellers on dangerous roads, often charged a toll whether there was really any danger or not. Some Templars were said to have become lax in their religious obligations, and it was also suggested that they drank to excess, wenched and generally behaved in a way that denigrated their illustrious foundation.

As the saying goes, "every barrel has its bad apples", and the Templar institution was almost certainly no exception. This period of European history was, of its essence, cruel and barbaric, no matter what one's station or class and the Templars were certainly hard men living in hard times. It is interesting, however, that despite the sort of rumours listed above, which probably proliferated at all levels of society at the end of the thirteenth century, we cannot discover a single case of an official complaint being made against a Templar knight to any overall authority such as that of the pope. This is not to suggest that we consider the Templars to be the paragons of virtue that certain modern sources would wish to believe they were. As in all such cases, the truth of the situation undoubtedly lies somewhere in the middle. However, it is equally important to see how well the Templars had held to their vows in the almost two centuries of their existence.

The Templars, despite their military strength, had never attempted to invade a Christian country, no matter how different its Christianity may have been from a totally orthodox kind. Indeed, during the Albigensian Crusade fought against the Cathar of southern France in the thirteenth century, the Templars, though involved, showed a marked preference to stay clear of what amounted to genocide on behalf of the Christians. And this despite the fact that the pope specifically and absolutely sanctioned the invasion. Time and again in their campaigns in the Outremer, the Templars had shown themselves to be fearless fighters and had often won magnificent victories against all likelihood. The Templars were often at odds with other Christian military orders, such as that of the Hospitallers, but there is no record of open hostility of a physical nature having been promoted or prosecuted against any brother orders.

Beyond religion, the Templars had become shrewd businessmen and great merchants. They represented an institution not unlike the later British East India Company, except for the fact that they were not tied to any one ruler or state. So far as is known, they maintained their own democratic institutions and were respectful to the rulers within whose domains they were stationed, only straying from such a policy when deliberately threatened.

Templars regularly acted as mediators between warring national or baronial factions and supported bankrupt monarchies, even though the chances of them ever being properly repaid were slim. As far as France was concerned, it might be suggested that the Templars even contributed to their own downfall, since it was they who saved Philip IV from an angry mob baying for his blood in Paris. Philip was royally lodged at the Templars own presbytery until things quietened down. Despite this fact, he turned on the Templars with tremendous savagery in 1307, and would gladly have eradicated all trace of the order from the face of the world if it had been within his power to do so.

Chapter 18

The Annals of Infamy

At dawn on Friday, 13 October 1307, all the Templar properties that fell within the jurisdiction of the French crown were entered at the same time by representatives of Philip IV. According to contemporary reports, the men undertaking this exercise were working under orders that had been sealed until the previous night. The knights and servants of the order were roused from their beds and immediately taken into custody. Properties and lands were confiscated and, as much as was possible, escape routes from the French lands were blocked to prevent members of the order from slipping the net.

Interrogations began immediately. Nobody associated with the order was immune and one of the first casualties in Paris itself was Jacques de Molay, grand master of the entire Templar order. The grand master had been summoned to France on the pretext of important meetings with the French king and the pope, and supposedly with no idea of what laid in store for himself and his brethren. His torture seems to have commenced almost immediately. We can be certain that it was severe and protracted.

The charges brought against the Templars were mostly religious in nature and dealt with a supposed heresy. Most of the accusations are well-known to regular readers on Templar history, but since we did not specifically identify them in our book *The Warriors and the Bankers* we feel it is prudent to do so now. It was suggested that the Templars were guilty of the following:

1. The denial of Christ and defiling the cross.
2. The worship of an idol.
3. The performance of a perverted sacrament.
4. Ritual murder.
5. The wearing of a cord of heretical significance.
6. The use of a ritual kiss.
7. Alteration to the ceremony of the mass and the use of an unorthodox form of absolution.
8. Immorality.
9. Treachery to other groups of the Christian forces.

It is clear that the king of France could never have levelled such charges in the first place if he had not been on good terms with the pope of the period. After all, it was Church law, enforced by papal decree, that the Templar order was responsible to no temporal authority in the world, and that its ultimate responsibility was entirely and irrevocably to the pope himself. Philip would not have been so stupid as to ignore this fact, and the only reason he moved against the Templars in 1307 was that he "owned" the papacy at the time.

This turn of events is absolutely pivotal to Philip IV's ultimate ability to attack the Templars, and the story probably began back in 1294 with the election of Pope Boniface VIII (original name Benedetto Caetani). Boniface spent most of his nine years as pope in bitter feuds with Philip IV. There were many reasons for the arguments, but uppermost was the old chestnut about who controlled the clergy, the Church or the State. Philip went further, and together with Edward I of England (a monarch with whom he had absolutely nothing else in common), he decided to tax the clergy. Boniface could not accept this insult and a long and bitter struggle ensued. Philip managed to stir up trouble time and again in Italy, and towards the very end of the rule of Boniface VIII, the king of France plotted in the kidnapping of the old man. Boniface, who was on the verge of excommunicating Philip, was cruelly treated and, though released, he died soon after, a broken man.

The next pope, Benedict XI (original name Niccolo Boccasini) reigned for only a year. He tried hard to heal the rifts between Philip IV and the Vatican, but he refused to absolve Philip's agents or Italian co-conspirators from blame concerning the death of his predecessor. It is now commonly accepted that he was poisoned by Italian factions allied to the French king.

In the meantime Philip had managed to ensure that the majority of cardinals in the Vatican were either French or else supporters of the French cause. As a result, he was able to ensure that with the death of Benedict XI, the next pope, and several after, would be of French blood.

The first of these was Bertrand de Got, who was elected in 1305 at Perugia as Pope Clement V. He was a Frenchman and, though history has often tried to do him justice by suggesting that he tried hard to elevate and consolidate the papacy, in reality he was in the hands of the French crown throughout the whole of his tenure. This fact stirred up so much animosity in Rome that in 1309 he transferred papal authority from Rome to Avignon in French territory. Philip's careful planning was bearing fruit. Throughout the reigns of Boniface VIII and Benedict XI, it would have been absolutely impossible for Philip to make his legendary attack on the Templars, at least with any hope of securing the all important backing of the Vatican. Clement was a different kettle of fish altogether, and in any case it is likely that the fate of his two predecessors was never far from his mind.

Ever since the start of our co-operation into Templar research, we as co-authors have found it impossible to believe that Philip's attack on the Templar order took the organization anywhere near as much by surprise as orthodox historians have tended to assert. At the start of the fourteenth century, the Templars still represented the strongest and richest independent force in the western Europe of their day. Their very organization, spread as it was like the roots of some huge plant through the soil of Europe and beyond, offered them ample opportunity to remain in touch with all the political machinations of their day. It is certain that they maintained agents in every royal court and that they had the ear of ruling baronial elites, whose sons after all formed the backbone of their own organization.

Critics to our point of view have been few in number, but those who did demur have asked the question: If all of the Templars knew that they were about to be attacked by the French throne, why did their grand master, Jacques de Molay, so willingly travel to France in 1307, knowing that he would end up in chains?

This is a fair question to consider and we recognize two possible answers:

Either

1. Jacques de Molay underestimated Philip's power to manipulate the pope, who in 1307, was still ensconced in Rome. He may therefore have considered that his own capture, if it took place at all, would have been of short duration, and that his cause would have prevailed ultimately.

Or

2. Conversely, Jacques de Molay may have been very much more astute, and is likely to have foreseen exactly what was ultimately destined to happen to his order. His trip to Paris takes on an entirely different series of possibilities if this is the case. And the most likely explanation, borne out by what we know of the Templars after this time, is that Jacques de Molay made himself a willing sacrifice to the intentions of Philip IV.

Many of the Templar knights interrogated and tortured by Philip's well-trained thugs were young and inexperienced, just the sort of men who could be prevailed upon to say anything merely to stop the agonizing torture and the threats of an ignominious and violent end. Even the bravest and hardest of warriors could be forced down roads they would not willingly travel normally so that Jacques de Molay, seasoned warrior that he was, found himself putting his name to all manner of confessions that he would eventually retract.

Philip IV may have managed to convince himself that the Templars were an "infected" order, and we will show that, at least to some extent, his suspicions were correct (at least within the precepts of the period). However, what other motivations lay behind his actions?

Philip was habitually short of money and had been since the very start of his reign. As if the depleted coffers of France had not been sufficiently drained by the constant warring of his father Philip III, Philip IV himself became involved in costly wars with his neighbours, not least of all England. He knew the Templars to be tremendously rich, even within France. His earlier enforced stay within the Templar presbytery in Paris had reconfirmed his belief that they were sitting on vast quantities of gold and silver. Philip owed the Templars a huge amount of money, and it would have been very plain to him that with the end of the Templars this debt would be immediately wiped out. In addition, he would come into possession of all French Templar treasure and lands.

The Templars were the largest international financial association of the period, with power enough to even set a gold standard for much of Europe. This restricted Philip's power within his own lands and forced him into relationships with other nations, which he did not relish. This was after all the beginning of the age of "the divine right of kings". Any monarch, specifically placed on the throne by God himself, was hardly likely to take kindly to following economic policies brought about by some outside agency such as the Templars.

Perhaps these facts would have been incentive enough, but there was undoubtedly more to the situation than hard cash and future economic policy. Early in Philip's reign, the West had finally been thrown out of the Holy Land, and most of the Templars garrisoned there had been brought back to other presbyteries in Europe, many of them in France. We have seen that there may have been up to 20,000 armed knights in the Templar order and a large percentage of them were living in Philip's own back yard. It is said that rumours abounded which pictured the Templars casting around anxiously for a piece of Europe that they could call their own. It has been suggested that Philip was afraid that this might ultimately have proved to be a part of his domains, probably the south of France. Even if the Templars had managed to bring all their fighters to France, they could hardly have matched the might of the army that Philip could muster, but things certainly would not have been quite so simple.

Anyone in medieval times, who had sufficient cash, could buy themselves an army of mercenaries which, if spearheaded by Templar knights, would have represented a formidable foe even against mighty France. Philip was naturally suspicious, almost paranoid on occasions, and he may well have believed that such rumours regarding the Templars were based on fact.

It is also known that Philip had sought a kind of honorary enrolment to the Templar order, and that he had been ignominiously refused. This final indignity might have been enough for him to convince himself that the Templars had to go.

With regard to the specific charges made against the order, history generally comes down on the side of believing that they were all fabricated and merely represented an excuse for the destruction of the Templar order. We are not entirely sure that this is the case. Of course, as human beings, we could never condone the type of treatment meted out to the captured Templars. However, there is some evidence that, at least within the Roman Catholic dogma of the period, the Templars were a heretical sect. Whether their divergence from accepted dogma made them "better" than orthodox Catholics of their day is not really the issue. But we have shown that Templarism, like the original Cistercianism, sprang from a religious fountain that was already many thousands of years old, before the Carolingian-inspired Roman Catholicism even existed.

We remain convinced that many of the ancient beliefs of the people who had formed and nourished the Templar movement at its birth remained in place within the order. We are further satisfied that it was the perpetration of these beliefs that offered Philip some sort of stick with which to beat the Templars.

Proof against the Templars, in the sense that it would be recognized in medieval France, was very different from the sort of proof that would be demanded in any court of law today. In effect, the Templars were guilty from the moment the instructions to arrest the order and seize its property were issued. We can see time and again that in such societies as the England and France of the period, charges tended to be brought, and then evidence was either elicited or invented to ensure the desired result. In assessing the true guilt or innocence of the Templars, it is necessary to look at subsequent evidence only available at a later period which was even then suspect because of the sources from whence it emanates.

The true religious observance and the daily rituals that took place in Templar presbyteries are never going to be known to the modern world. Therefore, despite our own beliefs regarding the Templars and their truly ancient pedigree, it is certain that Philip IV's case is never going to be unequivocally proved or disproved. As far as the evidence put forward at the time is concerned, virtually none of it would stand up to modern legal scrutiny. Most confessions of guilt were extracted under torture; material proof was fragmentary; and documentary proof more or less non-existent. The confession of specific Templar brothers is interesting, but since they were elicited under duress, they would never be considered to be admissible evidence today. Nevertheless, the statements made by some of the tortured personnel may give us a window into the organization, the internal structures of which remain otherwise unknown.

For example, several confessions revolved around the supposed worship by Templars of a mysterious bearded head, which was referred to as "Baphomet". Argument has raged for decades as to what Baphomet actually represented. Some researchers have suggested that the name was merely a corrupted form of the name "Mohammed", chief prophet of the Muslim religion. The inference is that the Templars had spent so long in the company of Muslims that their own Christian beliefs had become "infected" by non-Christian, Islamic doctrines. This assumption really doesn't hold much water for one important reason. No Muslim "worships" Mohammed, and such a notion would be repulsive to the Islamic mind. Only God is worthy of veneration, whilst Mohammed, though deeply important, is recognized as being a man and therefore distinct from the godhead. Graven or pictorial images, especially regarding the Prophet, would be equally repugnant to this faith. If the Templars really had been deeply affected by the values of Islamic religion, they would have been well aware of these facts.

A much more likely explanation is supplied courtesy of the work of the late Dr Hugh Schonfield. He was one of the experts who toiled for years interpreting parts of the Dead Sea Scrolls. During his work, he came across a Hebrew code, which he referred to as the "Atbash Cipher". This code had been used as a means for concealing the names of individuals within the documents. Dr Schonfield eventually came to believe that the Templars had known the Atbash Cipher and actively used it. This realization would not surprise us as much as it might some researchers, because we have already demonstrated our belief that at least some ancient texts from the Holy Land were in the possession of those who created the Templar order.

If the word Baphomet is subjected to the Atbash Cipher, the resulting word is "Sophia". What makes this particularly interesting is the derivation of the word Sophia in the context of Christianity. *Sophia* is a Greek word which literally translated means "wisdom". The gender root of the word is difficult to establish, but Sophia is the name that used to be given to the third component of the "Holy Trinity" in the early Christian Church. Therefore, in early Christian terms, the Trinity could be defined as, "The Father, The Son and Sophia" (or wisdom), in place of the more common and modern "Holy Spirit". In this context, Sophia has been seen by some agencies as a "feminine" concept. It has been further suggested, that with the "masculinization" of the third component of the Trinity, the Virgin Mary began to be venerated in order to fill the gender vacuum that had developed at the heart of Christianity.

We would argue that one of the factors that separated the Cistercians and the Templars from orthodox Christianity of their day was their huge reliance on the "feminine" within the godhead. This was expressed in several ways. We have seen that St Bernard himself was committed, absolutely, to the figure of the Virgin Mary. This is reflected in Cistercianism, in which each and every abbey was dedicated to her name. St Bernard had undergone mystical experiences regarding Mary, and had urged the Vatican to "regularize" and "elevate" her position within the Church.

Much emphasis these days is placed upon the Templars' own regard for St John the Baptist, and it has been suggested that the bearded head, sometimes associated with the name Baphomet, was meant to represent John. However, from the very inception of the Templar order, the real religious motivation was with regard to Mary. The Templar order was dedicated to her name and service, and it was her name that the knights cried as they went into battle. We hope to show that this carefully hidden feminine component of the godhead is clearly reflected in post-Templar organizations such as Rosicrucianism and Freemasonry. However, its inclusion in these bodies is as veiled to the average initiate as it would have been to the low-ranking Templar brother. It is likely that the French inquisitors never understood what Baphomet was meant to represent or, that if they did, they were quite happy to ignore the implications.

In our estimation, the most likely explanation is that the bearded head and Baphomet were either deliberately confused by Templar agencies or the whole situation was completely misunderstood by low-ranking Templar representatives, and their admissions under torture reflected this fact.

Several Templar brothers were said to have admitted defiling the crucifix, either by spitting or stamping upon it. There is no way of testing these claims adequately. On balance, this kind of behaviour seems to be absolutely opposed to what we know of the Templar order and its avowed beliefs. There may just be echoes of early Cistercianism inherent in such practices, but not because of any lack of reverence for Jesus himself. The Cistercians, and most especially St Bernard of Clairvaux, would not allow crucifixes, in the accepted sense of the word, into their churches. All that adorned the altar was a plain, wooden cross, which is not the same thing as the cross with Jesus *in situ*. However, such arguments may be semantic.

Another possible reason for this practice, if indeed it happened at all, could be associated with the "age" of the Christian religion. One young Templar knight is reported to have told a story of his initiation. He alluded to an incident in which he was shown a crucifix by an older Templar brother. The young man was instructed, "Do not have faith in this, it is too young". The most likely reason for this strange statement would seem to be that the older man was alluding to a certain knowledge on behalf of the Templars, that what the order knew sprang from something that predated Christianity by a long period. We could hardly find fault with such an assertion, since this is the very point of view to which we have been continually drawn during our investigations. But a statement such as this is a far cry from actively "defiling" such a sacred Christian symbol. It is just conceivable that a statement such as "Do not have faith in this, it is too young", was taken out of context in some areas of Templarism, and that this ultimately led to abuse of the sacred object. This is not an entirely satisfactory explanation but it might go some way towards explaining such strange behaviour (assuming, of course, that it ever really took place).

There is absolutely no satisfying evidence that the Templars ever took part in ritual murder, but since the accusers were clearly trying to imbue the order with demonic practices, it isn't surprising to find this accusation included on the list.

One or two of the charges are particularly interesting and may well be based on fact. For example, the use of a ritual kiss would be borne out by subsequent interpretations of the Templar induction ritual. However, these appeared at a later date and may be unreliable. But whether or not we believe that such a practice was present in Templar initiation, it is hard to see it as a justifiable reason for destroying an entire order. It was frequent practice in the Catholic Church, for example, for perfectly mainstream practitioners of the faith to kiss the ring of a bishop, a cardinal or a pope. However, since it was asserted at the trials that the Templars kissed each other on the mouth, or even on the buttocks, the inference is quite different. It is equally possible that this is another example of a perfectly innocent practice, being perverted by the excesses of the inquisitors who were determined to obtain confessions, no matter what the price.

We can find no specific accounts of the supposed "perverted sacrament" that is also included on the list of charges. In this regard, Alan had written extensively on the personal understanding that those of the Salt Line families may have had regarding the sacrament and what its specific implications may have been to its first practitioners. Once again though, to a crown that was determined to have its way, the slightest deviation from orthodoxy in the mass would have been enough to create more ammunition for the accuser's case.

It can be seen, then, that the majority of charges levelled at the Templars in 1307, and subsequently, relate specifically in one way or another to the form of Christian service being practised in the Templars own churches. We do not know what went on in the inner sanctum of Templar establishments at the start of the institution, nor right through until the fourteenth century. The Templars were responsible only to their own authority, and remained so for very nearly two centuries. Even today, secret societies, by their very nature, attract accusations of the most peculiar sort, and it is our experience that most of these are without the slightest foundation. Nevertheless, 200 years without regulation from some outside Christian agency is a long time. The Templar order was an insular, single-sex institution with a *raison d'être* radically different to that of most other Christian groups. The legacy of Templarism, which we maintain can be perceived in at least some aspects of Freemasonry, would indicate that sections of the order certainly did have astrological, astronomical, esoteric and alchemical overtones. If this is so, then by the standards of fourteenth-century Europe, Templarism was certainly heretical and its members had done more than enough to earn themselves a place on the scaffold. It should be recalled that the eminent Italian astronomer Galileo, a full 300 years after the demise of the Templars, came within a hair's breadth of being burned at the stake himself simply for asserting that the Sun was the centre of the solar system. It was not difficult to fall foul of Roman Catholic Church dogma at any stage between the tenth and the eighteenth centuries.

Perhaps in the end none of the arguments are of much importance because Philip IV wished to destroy the Templar order, at least in France, and he had sufficient power to undertake the exercise. Guilt or innocence was academic when dealing with the caprices of medieval thrones. It is impossible to know what ordinary people thought about the proceedings. In a largely pre-literate society, we have no record of rank-and-file opinions. The lower and middle aristocracy, the element of society that might have been expected to support the Templars, was generally powerless to do so under the prevailing circumstances in France at the time. It is certainly this selfsame group that rallied to the Templar cause in successive centuries and who kept the memory of Templar ideals alive through the songs of the troubadours and the later Grail legends.

The question we now have to ask ourselves is this: Was Philip IV of France successful in his attempt to destroy Templarism, not only within France but also across Europe and the known world as a whole?

The answer is very surprising!

Chapter 19

The Aftermath

Within a very short period of time, both Philip IV of France and his tame pope, Clement V, were speeding up the process of destroying the Templars in totality. Philip wrote in the strongest terms to his English counterpart, Edward II, imploring him to arrest all Templars within his realms and to seize their property. Edward decided to investigate matters for himself though. Correspondence between the two monarchs, immediately after October 1307, shows that Edward II, at least initially, was astounded by the accusations and that he plainly refused to believe them. Ultimately, the pope wrote to Edward II in such strident terms that the young king was spurred into action.

We have looked at Edward's actions carefully, and it seems likely that when the monarch realized that the writing was on the wall for the Templar order, he decided to embark upon a course of action that would suit his own ends. Like his royal neighbour Philip IV, Edward II was habitually short of money. He must surely have reasoned that if the Templars in Britain were going to be abolished in any case, he could not be expected to return all their wealth and property to the pope, as he had been instructed to do. Indeed, there is a surviving letter from Edward to the pope that makes this fact absolutely clear.

The matter had more or less sauntered along in England between October 1307 and October 1309, by which time the pope was losing his patience. In a letter dated 4 October 1309 he showed his displeasure to Edward by writing:

Your conduct begins again to afford us no slight cause of affliction, in so much as it has been brought to our knowledge from the report of several barons that, in contempt of the Holy See, and without fear of offending the divine Majesty, you have, of your own sole authority, distributed to different persons the property which belonged formerly to those of the Temple in your dominions . . .

Obviously not overly impressed by the tone of this rebuke, the young Edward penned a short and pointed reply:

As to the goods of the Templars, we have done nothing with them up to the present time, nor do we intend to do with them aught but what we have a right to do, and what we know will be acceptable to the Most High.

Despite this, Edward made no real attempt to shield the Templars in his domains from the wrath of the pope and allowed interrogators from the Continent to question English Templar personnel. The imprisonment of the Templars took its toll and some of them died, particularly in the Tower of London. It was not until June 1310 that the investigations in England and Ireland were concluded in their first phase, at which time a declaration was made, which said, "that certain practices had crept into the order of the Temple, which were not consistent with the orthodox faith". This is as much as three years of exhaustive questioning of both Templars and other parties could establish. In every real sense, the case against British Templars was unproven.

By this stage, many of the French Templars, having been forced into confessions through the most barbaric torture imaginable, had been released or had entered religious houses of one sort or another. Having recovered their health, very many of them were publicly retracting their original statements. At the beginning of May 1310, these recanters were rounded up and brought before Philip IV. He was outraged by their behaviour, and on Tuesday, 12 May 1310, fifty-four of them were led out and executed. More Templars were executed at Sens and more still were imprisoned for life as unreconciled heretics.

In England things moved in a different way. Edward II eventually put the Templar matter entirely into the hands of the ecclesiastical authorities, and he also allowed members of the order of St Dominic to come to England to carry out necessary tortures. Throughout many long months, this or that ecclesiastical court heard evidence, mainly from third parties who had never been Templars themselves. Meanwhile, strenuous efforts were made to persuade the imprisoned brothers to admit their heresy.

Finally, in around June 1311, two or three confessions were forthcoming. All bore a striking resemblance to known confessions elicited earlier in France. Those making the confessions had their previous excommunications revoked and were received into the Church once more. Following this, first in small and then in larger groups, most of the remaining imprisoned Templars in England conceded to a kind of compromise. In agreeing to the best demands the inquisitors could elicit from them, the Templars publicly apologized for anything they "might have" done wrong previously, and avowed themselves henceforth to be good Christians abiding by the laws and dictates of the Church. For the king and the prelates of England this seemed enough. Some of the Templars passed into holy orders, others remained in prison for some time, and the majority were freed at their own surety of good behaviour henceforth. Very few Templar knights were executed in Britain as a whole, though quite a number died in prison or during torture. Some of those absolved as a result of the statement to which they had put their names were even given pensions by the State.

On 16 October of the same year, the pope convened a general council of the Church at Vienne, in France. For some reason, which is not at all clear, several of the French bishops of areas which had previously persecuted Templar brothers now openly spoke on their behalf. The bishops openly admitted the transgressions of the Templars, but expressed a desire that such a great institution, which had done so much good work for the faith, should be allowed to speak in its own defence before it was formerly suppressed.

Philip IV and his puppet pope were both outraged by this appeal. The pope declared that if nobody else would sanction the suppression of the Templars, he would take the job upon himself. Early the next year, he convened a private consistory which was attended only by French cardinals and other trusted lackeys. The pope then abolished the order of the Temple by an apostolical ordinance. Any Christian who wished to avoid excommunication, and ultimately the stake, was henceforth perpetually prohibited from entering the order of the Temple, from wearing its mantle, or even pretending to be a Templar. When the Great Seal was applied to this ordinance, the Templars, as an officially sanctioned arm of the Roman Catholic Church, ceased to exist.

As to the fate of the Templar grand master, Jacques de Molay, it falls to us to rectify a misconception that has recently been penned by writers with regard to the end of the official Templar story. Probably to make the story seem even more heroic than it actually was, it is currently popular to assert that Jacques de Molay only admitted the falsity of his previous confessions on the morning of his death. In fact, he had been doing so for some time, and had even suggested that if the cardinals and other holy men who accused him "wore cloth of any different sort", he would challenge them to single combat for the lies they had been telling. As a result, the authorities knew quite well what to expect from him, as he and three other high-ranking Templar officers were led in chains to the base of a raised platform overlooked by Notre Dame Cathedral in Paris.

There, on 18 March 1313, the Bishop of Alba read the previous confessions of the four knights aloud, and called upon them to renew their words and to purge their souls of the Templar heresy. The Templar visitor-general, Hugh de Peralt, taking the initiative, said that they would do whatever was expected of them. But the grand master raised his hand and spoke loudly to the crowd. No absolute record of his speech exists, but it is generally said to have gone as follows:

> I do confess my guilt, which consists in having, to my shame and dishonour, suffered myself, through the pain of torture and the fear of death, to give utterance to false-hoods, imputing scandalous sins and iniquities to an illus-trious order, which hath nobly served the cause of Christianity. I disdain to seek a wretched and disgraceful existence by engrafting another lie upon the original false-hood . . .

At this point, Jacques de Molay was interrupted by the other Templars present, who loudly pronounced his innocence. The Templars were quickly removed and taken back to their prison cells. Geoffrey (or Guy) de Chauney, Preceptor of Normandy, insisted on facing the same fate as his master, and so at dusk on the same day, they were once more led out from the darkness of the prison. Both men were slowly roasted to death, over charcoal fires, on a small island in the Seine close to the convent of St Augustine.

The papal decree ensured that all Christian countries in which Templar establishments had been founded would be obliged to try and convict Templars still present on their soil. As we shall see, in Germany the Templars were pronounced to be innocent of all charges, and in Scotland the Papal decree was followed, but never with more than half-hearted enthusiasm. Portugal declared the Templars to be innocent, and finding itself to be on the wrong side of the pope's decree, simply re-founded the order under a different name. Intensely Catholic Tarragona and

Aragon subjected its Templar knights to the full rigours of the Dominican inquisitors, but still found them to be blameless.

It is suggested, probably incorrectly, that Jacques de Molay, with his dying breath summoned both the pope and the king of France to appear with him before the throne of God within one year to account for their actions, at which time God would decide the right of the matter. Whether or not the assertion of this statement is true, both Philip IV and his tame pope were dead within a year. The pope was struck by a mysterious bout of dysentery, and the king died of a strange disease which nobody could either name or treat. Edward II, the king of England who had at first so strenuously defended the Templars, and then just as strenuously renounced them, met an even more grizzly fate when he was murdered in Berkeley Castle by means that were just as savage as those handed out to the unfortunate Templars.

During the long period of time between the attacks of 1307 and the killing of the grand master, the thrones of France and later England had ample time to take the various Templar presbyteries to pieces, stone by stone. This task was undertaken in order to recover the huge fortune that it was known the Templars controlled. By papal edict, it was decided that all former properties belonging to the Templars should pass into the hands of their arch rivals, the Hospitallers. In fact, this did happen in some cases, though much Templar land reverted to the crown, who on both sides of the English Channel disposed of it as they saw fit.

But search as they may, no trace was found of the vast wealth in gold and silver which supposedly had been seen in both the London and the Paris presbyteries prior to 1307. This state of affairs was made even stranger in the case of Paris. It was known that when Jacques de Molay was summoned there from the Mediterranean region in 1307, he had brought with him a huge sum of money in gold, which he had ostensibly deposited in the Templar Paris headquarters on his arrival. Some valuable objects were found there, but no substantial sum in gold or silver, which made Philip even more determined to have the grand master not only humiliated, but killed.

Armies of authors have written libraries of books speculating as to where the Templar treasure might have gone. Innumerable expeditions have been launched, to all manner of places, with the express intention of locating the Templar hoard.

Our common approach to this problem differed markedly from that of the "treasure seekers". As fellow writers on the Templars and researchers of long standing, we discovered almost immediately that we shared the same opinion regarding almost all Templar wealth. These matters we have dealt with extensively in our book, *The Warriors and the Bankers*. However, the money specifically brought to Paris by Jacques de Molay is a different matter and one that we have examined particularly closely during recent months. Regarding the disappearance of this gold, the theory which seems most likely to be correct is one that was propounded by our friend and fellow researcher, John Ritchie. John believes that almost as soon as the treasure arrived in Paris, it was transferred to the Paris headquarters of the Knights Hospitallers, in lieu of payment for a transaction they were about to undertake on behalf of the Templars. John Ritchie believes that the money was intended to pay for the purchase of the island of Rhodes.

This assertion may not be half as unlikely as it at first sounds. Critics will argue that there was absolutely no love lost between the Templars and the Hospitallers. Despite these assertions, there is not a single case of either order drawing its swords in anger against the other. It is true that the pope had endeavoured to persuade the Templars to unite with the Hospitallers, and that they had refused to do so, but the reasons Jacques de Molay offered for this refusal seem eminently reasonable. Amongst other factors, he suggested that the honest rivalry between the two institutions could only be a good thing for both. If for example, the Hospitallers sent more fighting men to the Middle East in any given year, the Templars would be sure to outdo them in the following year. By this means, Christian pilgrims were twice as likely to be safeguarded as they went about their lawful business. In any case, Jacques de Molay also pointed out that he was not at liberty to commit Templar property to any merger of this sort, since to do so would have been to contradict the wishes of those many hundreds of sponsors who had so generously given land and money to the Templars. There was, explained the grand master, no way to know if dead patrons would have objected to such a merger.

Of course, behind these objections we can perceive other considerations, not least of all the fact that a merger with the Hospitallers would undoubtedly have alerted the secular and religious leaders of Europe to the true wealth of the Templar order – which in the heady atmosphere of the late thirteenth century would not have been prudent from a Templar point of view.

However the Knights of St John of Jerusalem, the correct title of the order referred to as the Hospitallers, are generally reported as having settled themselves on the Greek island of Rhodes after 1309. In the ensuing centuries, they made the island into a virtually impregnable fortress, until they were finally driven out in the sixteenth century. It is known that the Templars were looking for a new base of operations after their losses in the Holy Land at the very end of the thirteenth century. They had previously tried to settle on Cyprus, but had been unsuccessful for a number of reasons. If, as we have previously suggested, the Templars knew that the writing was on the wall for them in Europe, they may well have considered Rhodes to be an ideal location and a place that they could call their own. Rhodes occupies an unparalleled position in terms of both the Aegean and the Mediterranean, and it also guards the southern approaches to the Black Sea.

We have to ask ourselves if it is entirely plausible that the Hospitallers, a much less wealthy institution than the Templars, would in 1309 have had the financial wherewithal to purchase Rhodes and then to so rapidly build the huge fortresses with which it became justifiably famous. In addition, we are put in mind of the existence of a later order of chivalry, known as the Order of the Golden Fleece, which will be discussed fully in the second part of this book. The Order of the Golden Fleece was almost certainly a post-Templar chivalric offshoot, not a Hospitaller one, and in its Classical associations was particularly relevant to Rhodes.

Of course, there is no absolute proof that the large sum of gold Jacques de Molay brought with him to Paris was intended for the purpose of purchasing Rhodes, or that it ended up with the Hospitallers who used it themselves to this end. It is clear that Jacques de Molay refused to merge his order with that of the Knights of St John when prompted to do so by the pope and the king of France, but that does not necessarily infer that he would have failed to consider such an action on his own terms.

The relationship between the two orders may have been somewhat closer than is usually realized, especially in the late thirteenth century. There is, for example, some evidence that the former Templar lands in Scotland, which passed subsequently to the Hospitallers, were never "taken" by them, but merely "held in trust". This would infer an understanding regarding the Temple on the part of the Hospitallers and perhaps a hitherto little understood co-operation.

We have no way of knowing the composition of the Hospitaller knights who were destined to garrison Rhodes, but they were well beyond the political and military influence of both Church and State in Europe. Rhodes would have made an ideal bolthole for some of the Templar knights and staff who had escaped the snare of the pope and his fateful edict. We do not suggest Rhodes as the primary candidate for a post-Templar homeland (we have a far better candidate), but John Ritchie's theory cannot be ruled out and we hope to keep researching the issue in the hope of turning up more substantial evidence.

This particular treasure aside, as Templar researchers we are left with the puzzle of what happened to the vast majority of Templar wealth, which was never seized by the king of France, or any other monarch for that matter. Philip was furious that all

the gold and silver he was sure must be stored in Templar establishments throughout France had escaped his grasp – but this
may be because he simply failed to understand what the
Templar empire was really all about.

In their banking enterprises, merchant shipping, tax
collecting, farming and general transportation, the Templars
resembled a large multinational company. In *The Warriors and
the Bankers*, we rather irreverently called them "Templar Inc.",
though we are cognizant that "Templar International Ltd" might
be an even more apt description. Every economist, and even
most of us unskilled in economic knowledge, knows where the
treasure of a large multinational resides. Let us suggest that for
some reason the suddenly avaricious authorities of any western
European state, or perhaps the USA, was to raid all the offices
of the IBM Corporation. The investigating officers would be
very unlikely to find huge piles of dollar bills gathering dust in
the basement. In an economy such as that enjoyed at present by
the Western world, money is made to work. And if this is true
with regard to a corporation such as IBM, it is equally true of a
large international bank. Of course, the branches of every bank
have to keep sums of money in their vaults, but as a percentage
of the "worth" of the entire banking institution, this is
absolutely tiny. Banks flourish and grow because they invest
money.

If every depositor of any of the biggest world banks suddenly
decided to withdraw the amount that is entered into their
passbook on the same day, the whole network would collapse
within hours. The key word is "trust", and it is this that keeps
capitalism running more or less smoothly. To medieval Europe,
all of this would have been a complete mystery because money
wasn't treated in this way. But the Templars had come as close
to understanding these facts and to implementing them as any
organization prior to their period. They were lenders on a
massive scale, and were constantly spending money updating
their fleets, farms, fighting units and the like. A king, such as
Philip IV, who was used to keeping treasuries in secure castles,

with massive security, knew little about using money in this way. It has to be suggested therefore, though it might not be entirely romantic to make such an assertion, that no Templar treasury was found because, at least in the way that was expected, none existed.

This is not to suggest that each major Templar city holding throughout Europe would fail to put its hands on large amounts of cash if it were necessary to do so, but Templar International was a vibrant, working, expanding, trusting series of enterprises. It is surely clear that most of its financial assets were tied up in the various strands of commerce that were its lifeblood.

That kings such as Philip IV borrowed money, there is no doubt, but as to their understanding of the sheer depth of Templar interests, we are not so sure. Philip would have soon discovered that to try and gain liquid assets from Templar International was about as easy as trying to take the flour out of a cake once it is cooked and on sale in the confectioner's shop. In other words, the sheer chemistry of capitalism ensures that such a widespread enterprise would have to be taken to pieces very carefully across a long period of time and with the full co-operation of its operatives in order to recoup its actual worth. Philip was the king of France, but the many twisted tendrils of the Templar enterprises reached well beyond the frontiers of his domains. He may indeed, in his peremptory attack on the Templars, have instantly destroyed any hope of recouping a large proportion of Templar wealth.

Medieval monarch though he was, Philip IV was no fool and was said to be one of the most learned kings of the period. It is likely, therefore, that he understood at least some of the factors mentioned above. In fact, history tells us that he did, for he deemed it absolutely necessary not only to persecute French Templars, but to try and coerce other monarchs into doing exactly the same thing. In Germany, throughout large areas of the Iberian Peninsula, largely in Scotland, and all along the Baltic coast, he and the pope were singularly unsuccessful with this regard. To break off one leg, or even two, of an octopus does not necessarily mean the death of the creature, and if the octopus knows that it is under threat, it had better move out of the way altogether. The Templars were shrewd operators, with nearly 200 years of learning under their belts. To suggest that the 1307 attacks put paid to the order completely is to fail singularly in understanding the magnitude of the proposed task. It is also to ignore the depths to which Templar International was planted into the very earth of Europe and beyond.

It is certain that Templarism was severely damaged in the years after 1307. It is a fact that the institution had to split, diversify and give itself a multitude of new names. Templar lands in France, England and in a number of other states were gone for good. Its farms and churches were either taken by others or left to fall into ruin. The famous and formidable merchant and fighting fleets had to lower one flag and hoist another – and in some places it had to trade one segment of its product base to preserve others. However, when one looks closely at the history of Europe after 1307, while understanding the careful and often devious operators who lay at the heart of the Templar phenomenon, it is quite clear that, in one form or another, Templarism survived. We are in no doubt that it continues to do so until the present day.

Chapter 20

The End of an Era

Of the fact that the Templar order, as it had been known for nearly 200 years, disappeared at the beginning of the fourteenth century there is no doubt. True it, reappeared in different places under altered names and perhaps it also survived to some degree within the ranks of the Knights of St John. However, "The Poor Knights of Christ and the Temple of Solomon" were ruthlessly and cruelly exterminated and hounded out of existence by a corrupt pope, a greedy and cruel king and a number of compliant monarchs throughout Europe. While Roman Catholicism held sway in the Western world, it would have been absolutely impossible for Templars to raise their heads above the parapets as "Templars" and hope to keep them attached to their bodies.

In other words, if Templarism did survive, it had to either hide or change. This process would have been made very much easier if there was in 1307, and had always been, an institution underpinning Templarism, but which existed independent of it. We believe that there was, and that it survived the vicissitudes of the fourteenth century.

Our journey has been a long one, so it is worth looking briefly again at the continuum. Starting our search in the mists of prehistory, we have demonstrated that the standard world view of the neolithic period in Europe revolved around a belief in a "balanced" male/female deity. This seems to have led to an equitable and probably reasonably peaceful period for its adherents. If the case for Minoan Crete is to be believed, life was extremely peaceful in the period leading up to around 2000 BC, though circumstances obviously differed from place to place.

Events in the Middle East were to change dramatically for a number of reasons beyond this important historical watershed. Whether as a result of a natural event, the eruption of Santorini sometime around 1750 BC, or for more complex reasons, the old neolithic religions and way of life began to disappear.

The primary reason for these changes revolved around the arrival of warlike peoples from further afield. The need for self-defence led to a more martial view of life generally, and seems to have thrust upon the people of the time the adoption of a "male-dominated" religious imperative. This was later modified to a religious model that considered God to be not only male, but also "single" and "unique". Thus religions such as Judaism were gradually born.

Meanwhile, the old neolithic imperative, epitomized most strongly in the megalithic cultures of the far west, went into a decline, but there is good evidence that it never died. Even within the Judaic worldview, there was room for factions such as the Essene. Some of these groups had a far more complex view of the cosmos and of religion than the one that seems to be espoused by orthodox Judaism as we see it today. Meanwhile the early kings of Israel, such as Solomon, can be shown to have been of a radically different religious inclination than the much later Old Testament of the Bible generally infers.

The megalithic genius, legacy of neolithic Europe, flourished in Britain and France, evolving a worldview that was more complete and more complex than anything that would surface again until seventeenth-century Europe. Paramount in the retention of this way of thinking were the Celts. The Celts were an ancient group of peoples from Germany and Switzerland who invaded Britain and France during the Iron Age. They were more warlike and fractious than the megalithic peoples had been, but they were of the same basic stock and they seem to have retained many of the religious imperatives of a much earlier period.

Inheriting at least some of the megalithic knowledge, the spiritual leaders of the Celts, the Druids, kept alive knowledge of the Salt Line system laid down back in the Bronze Age. They revered Salt Line sites and created new ones. No European race was absolutely insulated from the Bronze Age inheritance, and it could be seen emerging time and again, particularly in the various "mystery religions" that predominated prior to and even after the emergence of Christianity.

The arrival of post-Constantine Roman Christianity did little to systemize existing belief in the West; it merely overlaid it with a veneer of state control. In fact Churches, whilst paying lip service to the needs of Rome, continued to practise their own, often distinct forms of Christianity, in some cases well into the eleventh century. Claims that the seventh century Synod of Whitby changed this state of affairs in Britain are not born out by the evidence. Christianity in Britain, and probably in Ireland too, had been much affected by Essene-type arrivals, with the destruction of Judea by the Romans in AD 70 and by Druidic thought. Until the arrival of Carolingian feudalism and Roman Catholicism, British and Irish Christianity remained schismatic and perhaps even heretical. In England especially, this can be shown to be at least partly the case until after the Norman Conquest of 1066.

During this period, people still existed who understood the megalithic worldview, religion and social organization. These selfsame people represented elements of the low and middle-ranking aristocracy inherited by the Carolingian monarchs. Most of the families in question had lived for centuries on the old Salt Lines. Forced into ever more stifling constraints by a political system they did not espouse, and by religious forms they could not adopt, they began to take a unique stance against prevailing norms and ruling dynasties.

Matters seem to have come to a head around the middle of the eleventh century, at which time the subterranean power of the Salt Line families began to exert itself. This group was certainly not large enough to try and retake Europe by storm. However, it was clever enough to understand that covert activity can be very successful. Instead of confronting feudalism and Roman Catholicism, the Salt Line families embraced it – and having gained themselves a strong position at the heart of both, they began to influence all manner of events.

The available evidence shows that this tendency was best exemplified within the borders of Burgundy, a kingdom originally founded by megalithic peoples from the island of Bornholm in the Baltic. Long before the existence of a single and unified France, the greatest flowering of this subversive genius emerged in the Salt Line city of Troyes, in Champagne. Champagne had originally been part of Burgundy and retained good relations with it. The people behind this movement we have named the Troyes Fraternity. To them, we credit the idea of the First Crusade, together with the formation of both the Cistercians and the Templars. It appears to have been their ultimate intention to side-step the importance of Rome as a religious institution. The capture and control of Jerusalem, the heart of Judaic and Christian belief, would gradually erode the power of Rome and its Catholic popes. Meanwhile they infiltrated the Vatican and forced measures to be taken that would safeguard their own particular religious values and practices. In particular they re-elevated the "feminine" at the heart of Christianity.

In order to gradually destroy the iron hard grasp of the feudal system, the Troyes Fraternity instituted a new form of monasticism. In a short time, the Cistercian ideal was backed up by the strongest and most cohesive fighting force that the Western world had ever seen up to that point – namely the Templars. The minds behind these schemes were shrewd and clever. They played ruler against ruler, faction against faction. For 200 years, they worked at destroying feudalism from within. The Troyes

Fraternity created a cohesive infrastructure of production, and then also instituted markets to deal with the produce. At base, the whole process depended upon the humble sheep, an idea that went back to Minoan Crete at the most golden age of the flowering of Bronze Age society.

A mixture of natural human greed and a series of unfortunate occurrences conspired to erode the power of the Troyes Fraternity and its various components towards the end of the thirteenth century and at the start of the fourteenth. In the end, the loss of Troyes and Champagne necessitated the relocation and rebuilding of the whole shadowy group. By the time the death knell sounded for the Templars, it is very likely that their masters were already out of the direct control of any European monarch, or that of the established Church.

This, in brief, is the story as we see it. In *The Warriors and the Bankers* we demonstrated some of the boltholes that the Templars, and presumably those who really ran the organization, had prepared for themselves once the writing was on the wall. Chief amongst these was the nation-state we today know as Switzerland. In Part 2 of the *The Knights Templar Revealed* we will return to this theme, examining the evidence base as it stands presently.

On the way through this long and fascinating story, we have attempted to answer many tricky questions. Many more still remain. For example: Did the ruling faction of the Templars and the Cistercians actually know about their origins in Bronze Age Europe? In answer to this question, we both shout a resounding "yes", though we must admit that to offer incontrovertible proof for this point of view may always be beyond our ability. That this knowledge was present around the time of St Bernard of Clairvaux, we have absolutely no doubt whatsoever and we hope our rehearsing of his life and imperatives has proved the fact beyond doubt. St Bernard of Clairvaux remains, in our minds, probably the most important man who ever lived in western Europe.

In our research, we are quite aware that there have been times when we have approached the conclusions of other writers. These include Baigent, Leigh and Lincoln, with their assertion that a group known as the Prieure de Sion has affected and still does affect the development of western Europe. In many respects our proposed Troyes Fraternity has much in common with the supposed Prieure de Sion. However, the attentive reader of both theories will note that there are major departures too.

In *The Warriors and the Bankers* we dealt, albeit in a fairly truncated way, with the possible direction taken by post-Templar thinkers. Part 2 of *The Knights Templar Revealed* will pick up those themes in the light of more complete and even more compelling evidence which is now coming to hand.

Did the Troyes Fraternity manage to survive the loss of its city and region? Did Templarism genuinely give way to Rosicrucianist alchemical study and latterly Freemasonry? Could it be argued that the whole Reforming movement of Christianity, which began to tear Europe apart in the sixteenth century, was deliberately instigated by the same cohesive group which created the Cistercians and the Templars? All these questions deserve to be fully addressed and we are presently already occupied with this task.

Slowly but surely, the full tapestry of history displays its intricate stitching and rich colours. Occasionally, the pictures the various strands create are surprising and some eyes refuse to accept the reality of the scenes that present themselves. The golden thread that showed itself briefly as Templarism disappeared behind the surface numerous times between the Bronze Age and the eleventh century, and for a while it was hidden from view when the Templars were attacked. However, we hope to show that it re-emerged, as lustrous and vibrant as ever, diversifying and multiplying.

We are all occasionally inclined to view the worst excesses of a world we sometimes think of as being barbaric and cruel. All the same, it is fair to say that most Westerners live in societies that are paragons of virtue and havens of independent thought in comparison with the feudalism of the medieval period. We have asked ourselves the question, how many of the advances we have made towards personal freedom came about as a result of post-Templar influence and thinking? We are forced to the conclusion that most of them did.

With regard to the revelations of this book, and the ones that wait for *The Knights Templar Revealed Part 2*, we make no apology for the surprise they engender, nor do we disguise the radical and subversive methods that many generations used to bring them into play.

Working together, we constantly marvel at how far the research has come. The merest mention of the very concepts with which we deal would have seen us rapidly committed to the flames only a few hundred years ago. We enjoy the freedom to research fully and to say what we find. That freedom was bought across centuries, and at a tremendous price.

The Troyes Fraternity, whatever they really called themselves, are at least partly responsible for the world we live in today. They risked much to retain something incredibly old, but wonderfully precious. Their story is a strange one, but it is very human.

All of us deserve to read the chapters of history. If some of the words are indistinct or missing, it is up to us to make the best guess possible. As the writers, Alan Butler and Stephen Dafoe, we can only apologize if our interpretation of the missing words of history is at variance with your own.

Selected Bibliography

C.G. Addison, *Knights Templars*, New York: Masonic Publishing, 1874

Michael Baigent, Richard Leigh and Henry Lincoln, *The Holy Blood and the Holy Grail*, London: Jonathan Cape, 1982

Michael Baigent and Richard Leigh, *The Temple and The Lodge*, London: Corgi, 1988

Malcolm Barber, *The New Knighthood*, New York: Cambridge University Press, 1994

Malcolm Barber, *The Trial of the Templars*, New York: Cambridge University Press, 1978

Bede, *Historia Ecclesiastica Gentis Anglorum*, London: Oxford University Press, 1996

E. Bonjour, H.S. Offler and G.R. Potter, *A Short History of Switzerland*, Oxford: Clarendon Press, 1952

Janet Bord and Colin Bord, *Ancient Mysteries of Britain*, London: Diamond Books, 1986

Robert Hewitt Brown, *Stellar Theology and Masonic Astronomy*, New York: D. Appleton, 1892

Edward Burman, *Supremely Abominable Crimes*, London: Allison & Busby, 1994

Alan Butler, *The Bronze Age Computer Disc*, London: Foulsham, 1998

Alan Butler and Stephen Dafoe, *The Warriors and the Bankers*, Ontario: Templar Books, 1998

Janet Burton, 'The Cistercian Adventure', in D. Robinson (ed.), *The Cistercian Abbeys of Britain – Far From the Concourse of Men*, London: Batsford, 1998.

John Chadwick, *The Decipherment of Linear B*, Cambridge: Cambridge University Press, 1990

Glyn Coppack, *The White Monks*, Stroud: Tempus, 1998

Stephen A. Dafoe, *Unholy Worship*, Ontario: Templar Books, 1998

Margaret Deanesly, *A History of the Medieval Church 590–1500*, London: Methuen, 1962

John Delaney, *Dictionary of Saints*, Kingswood: Kaye Ward, 1982

Peter F. Ellis, *The Men and Message of the Old Testament*, London: Liturgical Press, 1963

Robert Folz, *The Coronation of Charlemagne*, London: Routledge & Kegan Paul, 1974

Michael Foss, *People of the First Crusade*, New York: Arcade, 1997

Laurence Gardner, *Bloodline of the Holy Grail*, Shaftesbury: Element Books, 1996

George Goyau, *Saint Bernard*, Paris: Flammarion, 1927

Michael Grant, *Constantine The Great*, New York: Charles Scribner's Sons, 1993

Michael Howard, *The Occult Conspiracy*, Vermont: Destiny Books, 1989

B.S.J. Isserlin, *The Israelites*, London: Thames and Hudson, 1998

Christopher Knight and Robert Lomas, *The Hiram Key*, London: Arrow Books, 1996

Christopher Knight and Robert Lomas, *The Second Messiah*, London: Century Books, 1997

D. Knowles, *The Monastic Orders in England*, Cambridge: Cambridge University Press, 1963

Henry Lincoln, *Key to the Sacred Pattern*, Moreton-in-Marsh: Windrush, 1997

Donald A. Mackenzie, *Crete and Pre-Hellenic*, London: Senate, 1996

Albert Mackay, *The History of Freemasonry*, New York: Gramercy, 1996

F.A. Mourret, *A History of the Catholic Church Volume 3*, St Louis: Herder, 1936

Lynn Picknett and Clive Prince, *The Templar Revelation*, New York: Bantam, 1997

Albert Pike, *Morals and Dogma*, Washington: Roberts Publishing, 1871

Michael Prestwich, *Edward I*, New Haven: Yale University Press, 1988

Brian Pullan, *Sources for the History of Medieval Europe*, Oxford: Blackwell, 1971

John J. Robinson, *Born in Blood: The Lost Secrets Of Freemasonry*, New York: Evans, 1989

J.S. Romanides, *The Filioque, Anglican-Orthodox Joint Doctrinal Discussions St Albans 1975–Moscow 1976*, Athens: Athens Press, 1978

Earl of Rosslyn, Peter St Clair-Erskine, *Rosslyn Chapel*, Rosslyn: Rosslyn Chapel Trust, 1997

Desmond Seward, *The Monks of War*, London: Penguin, 1972

Joachim Schultz, *Movement and Rhythms of the Stars*, New York: Floris, 1963

Christopher Tyerman, *Who's Who in Early Medieval England 1066–1272*, London: Shepheard-Walwyn, 1996

Stephen Tobin, *The Cistercians*, New York: Overlook Press, 1995

Shirley Toulson, *The Celtic Year*, Shaftesbury: Element Books, 1989

Geza Vermes, *The Complete Dead Sea Scrolls in English*, London: Pelican, 1961

Index